Tabemasho!
Let's Eat!

A TASTY HISTORY OF JAPANESE FOOD IN AMERICA

Tabemasho!
Let's Eat!

Gil Asakawa

Stone Bridge Press • Berkeley, California

Published by
Stone Bridge Press
P. O. Box 8208, Berkeley, CA 94707
TEL 510-524-8732 • sbp@stonebridge.com • www.stonebridge.com

p-ISBN 978-1-61172-068-6
e-ISBN 978-1-61172-950-4

This book is dedicated to my father-in-law, Rex Yoshimura (1935–2021), who had a crystal-clear memory for great food, Japanese and otherwise, from long-closed restaurants he dined at decades ago, and who could name the best dishes at every current- and past-favorite eatery. He had great taste, and was an inspirational foodie before "foodie" was a thing.

Rest in peace.

Contents

Acknowledgments

This book would not have been possible without my mom's cooking, which instilled in me an appreciation of homemade Japanese food. My late dad was the griller of the family, and I owe my love of barbecues and grills of all kinds to him.

My wife, Erin Yoshimura, is a wellspring of Japanese cooking. She was raised in a Japanese American family that valued traditional cooking as well as Japanese American variations. What a wonderful partner to have in life! Erin's family also inspired me because her mom is an excellent cook and her late dad (to whom this book is dedicated) was not only a fastidious and expert griller but had an encyclopedic memory of Japanese restaurants and the best places for every kind of cuisine in Denver.

Erin and I still laugh about the first time I really understood the amazing cultural importance of Oshogatsu, when she and I got together and I attended my first-ever New Year's feast with her extended family and everyone's potluck contributions. I loved my small family's New Year's meals, but they were nothing compared to the wonderful Japanese and JA Yoshimura extravaganzas.

I also want to acknowledge the entire Japanese American community here in the Denver area, and nationally, for helping me embrace my JA roots and understand the history of our community in a more complete sense than just me and my memories of being a kid in Japan.

Thanks to my many friends on social media—especially Facebook, Instagram, and YouTube—who have liked, commented on, or messaged me about my #foodporn and #twEATs photos and encouraged me to do more to make my foodie passion something bigger.

Special thanks to Peggy Moore, Traci Chee, Jane Miyahara, Joseph Conti, Cay Fletcher, Eric Elkins, Laura Bloom, Randy Kirihara, and Randy Barbara Kaplan for sharing their experiences with Japanese food.

I look forward to many more great meals out, homecooked, and with all my family and friends. *Tabemasho!*

Gil Asakawa, August 2022

Introduction

I'm a foodie. I'm one of those annoying people who wait to eat at restaurants (and at home) just so I can take a nicely composed photo of the meal and post it with the hashtags #twEATs and #foodporn on social media. I like all kinds of food, from all over the world. I seek out new culinary experiences. My dining mantra is "if someone somewhere in the world eats something, I'm willing to try it . . . at least once."

But of all cuisines, Japanese food is my comfort food and ultimate palate pleaser. Japanese food, or *nihonshoku,* is a topic that's near and dear to my heart . . . and my stomach.

Of course, being born in Japan, I grew up eating Japanese food. My mom used to cook a lot of traditional Japanese dishes, but she made American food too: spaghetti and meat sauce, turkey on Thanksgiving, frozen TV dinners, and chicken pot pie or chicken a la king.

She always—*always*—had rice, *gohan,* at the table, whether the dinner was Japanese or not. And even if we had roast beef or spaghetti, she would often cook herself some salmon, which sometimes made for a clash of aromas in the kitchen. She'd shrug and have her *sake* (salmon, not rice wine, often pronounced "sha-keh") and gohan while my dad and brothers and I had beef, spaghetti, or whatever. In other words, I had a thoroughly bicultural upbringing.

As a kid, I paid close attention to my mom in the kitchen.

I noticed the subtleties of how she prepared meals and the rapid-fire chop-chop-chop of her slicing vegetables like green onions, carrots, or cucumbers—always at an angle—with her sharp *hocho* knife on the battered wood cutting board. I paid attention to the kinds of ingredients and spices, and the amounts she used (good thing, since she never wrote down proper recipes and couldn't tell you how much of each ingredient to use). I know about her vague recipes because when I went off to college, I was the son who asked her for them, most memorably her teriyaki sauce. "Heh? Just *shoyu*, sake, *mirin*, and shugah," she said bluntly (soy sauce, sake, mirin, and sugar).

I substituted beer for sake and mirin—hey, it was college!—and it worked OK, even if my mom wouldn't approve. I cooked a lot of teriyaki in college, and my roommate, who is Italian, made a lot of spaghetti sauce from scratch. We made a good team, and I learned about cooking from him, too. In college, I paid homage to my heritage—and my nascent foodie obsessions—when I hosted a weekly country rock show on the campus radio station, WPIR. For two hours on Monday nights, I mustered my coolest laid-back, low-voiced FM DJ voice and announced myself as . . . "Gil Asakawa, the Teriyaki Cosmic Cowboy." I cringe now when I think about it, but I thought it was pretty hip in the 1970s!

My wife, Erin Yoshimura, is a *yonsei*—fourth-generation Japanese American—who is more connected to her Japanese roots than most *sansei*, or third-generation JAs. She can read *hiragana* and *katakana* characters, which is something I can't do. Like me, she's a foodie who loves authentic Japanese cuisine. She cooks wonderful Japanese food, including JA dishes. Her parents cook lots of Japanese dishes too. Our family dinners and holiday get-togethers are a typical Japanese American mashup of cross-cultural deliciousness.

The first time I got to attend her extended family's Oshogatsu—New Year's—I was astounded at the *osechi ryori* spread that covered multiple tables in multiple rooms. Erin swears that's why I proposed to her—for the food. My mom would cook for a couple of days before the New Year and my folks would invite some friends over—the meal almost always had my mom making different kinds of sushi while my dad grilled steaks. But Erin's family celebration took many days of planning and cooking, and everyone contributed in a potluck spirit. There would be traditional New Year's dishes like *kuromame*, sweet black beans (eaten only in odd numbers for good luck), and there would be JA favorites like Spam *musubi*. Each New Year's Day morning we would eat my mother-in-law's savory *ozoni* soup, with pieces of soft mochi floating in it. Over the years I added my own contribution to the big family feast, a Yoshimura family recipe for *kakimochi*, buttery soy-sauce-and-sugar-coated crackers sprinkled with sesame seeds, which are made from, of all things, Tostitos tortilla chips.

Japanese cuisine is such a deeply rooted part of my being that I can't imagine living without it. I shudder to think what life would be like if Japanese food was entirely foreign and exotic here in the United States, the way it must have been in the early days of Japanese food in America.

I guess I'd have to satisfy my cravings by dreaming about the food of my childhood. Luckily, I've always had a great memory for food, and not just Japanese.

I have vivid, though somewhat mysterious, memories of a restaurant somewhere in Tokyo where my family would go for special meals of fancy sushi and other traditional Japanese fare. I must have been four or five years old, and I recall that my dad would drive us across town, then we'd have to walk some distance. I don't remember the name of the restaurant, but I have indelible images in my mind of the dark entrance hall into the dining room, which was lined with glass cases of samurai and ninja armor, masks, and weapons. I dreamed at that young age, like an American kid dreaming of owning a BB gun ("you'll shoot your eye out, kid!"), of being able to throw *shuriken* (ninja stars) with deadly accuracy.

I also have vivid memories of seeing men on bicycles precariously holding stacks—tall stacks—of lacquer boxes filled with *soba* noodles or bowls of ramen in one hand while they wove their way through crazy traffic and crowded alleyways, delivering food to hungry businessmen in Tokyo.

And I remember a favorite American food, freshly grilled hamburgers, from a food truck–like counter outside of an elementary school that my older brother and I attended in Iwakuni, on a Marine Corps base. That's when I first saw those plastic squeeze bottles with the conical tops, filled with ketchup and mustard. I loved those burgers. I think they were five or ten cents each.

Once we moved to America in the mid-1960s, I embraced all manner of American food, including, of course, fast food. McDonald's, Wendy's, Dunkin' Donuts, and Pizza Hut hadn't yet landed across the Pacific in Japan, so this was a whole new faux-food world for me. I embraced them all—my family would drive to a nearby town to have dinner out at the McDonald's there. We thought it was special. When a Jack in the Box opened a short walk from our suburban northern-Virginia home, I was in heaven. I still yearn sometimes—just once in a while—for a Jack in the Box taco, which was my first, albeit inauthentic, taste of Mexican food.

But Japanese food has always been my home base, my culinary nest—even when it was an unknown, a weird and exotic and sometimes just gross, cuisine in America.

When my family first moved to the States, Japanese food wasn't very available. My parents quickly sought out the lone Japanese grocery store in Washington, DC, where we would drive every weekend from northern Virginia to stock up on supplies for my mom to cook with (and snacks for me and my brothers to wolf down). On special occasions, we would go out to a couple of Japanese restaurants—more on that in a later chapter. Mostly, though, my mom cooked American food with ingredients from the local Safeway.

So it's amazing to see the cultural evolution—nay, *revolution*— that now has Japanese restaurants in every city and sushi in supermarkets across the US. Not just Asian or Japanese groceries, but giant American retail chains. I've heard six-year-old kids boast of how their family eats sushi a couple of times a week. Mind you, the sushi may not be the greatest, and the restaurants serving Japanese food may not exactly be paragons of authenticity. But they're symbols of how Japanese food has become accepted in America, and of how it's now considered mainstream.

1 Appetizer
An Introduction to the Japanese Pantry

Japan is a country surrounded by water—it's a large archipelago, with the main islands running from Hokkaido in the north down to Kyushu in the southwest and then on to the small island chain of Okinawa, which had been the Ryukyu Kingdom, influenced by Chinese culture, before it became part of Japan.

Because Japan is an island nation, of course seafood plays a huge part in Japan's food culture.

Many traditional dishes are simmered in *dashi*, a broth mainly flavored with a combination of seaweed and *katsuobushi*, shaved dried bonito, or dried sardines. This basic dashi is also used as the soup base for udon, hotpot, and more.

But Japan is also an agrarian country, with centuries of expertise in growing fruits, vegetables, and grains throughout the seasons and in all the different climates that the country encompasses, from the chilly winters of Hokkaido to the Hawaii-like tropical warmth of Okinawa. It comes as no surprise that rice was the main staple of the Japanese diet for centuries, along with vegetables and fish.

Wheat and especially buckwheat were also cultivated in Japan, along with barley and, of course, soy.

We all know about the samurai warriors (and the ninja and kimono-clad geisha that make up our collective image of old Japan). But the country and its culture are so much more than the images that come casually to mind, and so intertwined with influences from both Asia and the West, that, even in its culinary culture, Japan has absorbed much from outside its borders. To understand Japanese cuisine, it helps to look back at the history of food in Japan.

A brief history of beef in Japan

Historically, Japanese didn't eat much meat because of the predominance of Buddhism. Cows and cattle were considered draft animals, used for plowing the fields. Chicken and pork were served in some dishes, thanks in part to the influence of Chinese culture. The religious ban on meat wasn't absolute; people (most likely samurai, who needed strength to fight) were fed meat if they were sick, and meat was allowed to be cooked for certain rituals and celebrations. During the Edo period of isolation from the world, the eating of game animals, including boar and duck, was allowed. But no one asked, "where's the beef?"

So, what changed and made Japanese a carnivore's dream cuisine?

Foreigners came to Japan and influenced its food culture. Although Japan was officially closed off to the world during the Edo period from 1603 to 1867, Portuguese sailors first arrived in

1543 and established trade in Nagasaki in Kyushu, including selling Western guns to samurai clans. They also brought goods from China. Along with the traders, Portuguese Jesuit priests brought Christianity to southern Japan. But trade with Portugal diminished with the arrival of traders from another European country.

A Dutch ship landed in Kyushu in 1600, and in 1609 the Netherlands was granted trade status by Tokugawa Ieyasu, who had ruled Japan as a united country. He was interested in trade with the Dutch, but also liked that they were not so focused on missionary

"Always Been Part of My Life"
. . . .
Japanese food has always been a part of my life. Rice, tea and *tsukemono* with dinner were staples. Of course I would have loved to have more potatoes and pasta if it were up to me.

I have several favorite Japanese foods. Among my favorites are fresh mochi broiled then dipped in *shoyu* and sugar paste, *nabeyaki* udon, grilled fish, and *hamachi kama* with lots of oroshi. I like the simple flavors of fish and rice. The shoyu and sugar paste with grilled mochi makes a fun dessert or snack anytime.

Peggy Moore

work to convert Japanese to Christianity. They were allowed to trade during Japan's closed-off years, at the single port of Nagasaki. For more than two hundred years, only occasional shipwrecked Europeans washed ashore anywhere else.

But on July 8, 1853, Japan's society, culture, . . . and cuisine changed. Commodore Matthew C. Perry, an American naval officer sent by President Millard Fillmore to open Japan to trade with the United States, by force if necessary, arrived in Edo (the name for Tokyo until the Meiji Restoration in 1868) Bay and convinced the Japanese to begin the process of opening itself for business.

Along with the subsequent ascension of the Meiji Emperor came the country's embrace of all things European and American. Foreign experts were invited to help train Japanese professionals and establish modern industry, architecture, and food. As French cuisine was considered the pinnacle of sophistication, some of the most luxurious restaurants that served the incoming foreigners—a foreign settlement was established in Tsukiji, a Tokyo district that in a few decades would become known as the world's largest fish market—served French dishes. The head chef at the first Western-style hotel in Japan was a Frenchman, and he went on to run the kitchen at the Yokohama Grand Hotel before becoming the owner of a hotel in Kobe.

By the 1870s, Japan's Ministry of Education was explaining how to cook and serve Western-style food, which was called *yoshoku*, as opposed to traditional Japanese cuisine, called *washoku*. One flier printed by the government had an illustration of Western-style plate and cutlery, including a fork. The government thought that allowing a more Western diet would help the health of Japanese . . . and make them bigger.

As a sure sign of changing times, in 1872 the emperor hosted a New Year's celebration that included food influenced by European cuisine, including meat and eggs. The rush to westernize was on!

Soy beans, tofu, and soy sauce

The history of soy beans goes back even farther in Japan. Soy beans—in the form of salted, boiled-in-the shell edamame—have become familiar appetizers in the US, even outside of Japanese restaurants. Soy milk and tofu can be found in American supermarkets from coast to coast. Miso as a cooking ingredient, and in the ever-popular miso soup, is also a common item in grocery stores and restaurants.

Tofu, the ultimate product of soy beans, is popular as a side dish or main entree—it's a healthy, protein-packed meat alternative. The plastic cartons of the white bricks are easy to find in non-Asian grocery stores these days, and even in a membership warehouse chain like Costco. The rise of tofu, in part a parallel to the rise of Japanese food, is the result of America's passion for healthy lifestyles.

Like a lot of things that we consider Japanese, tofu originated in China and was brought to Japan by Zen Buddhist monks in the eighth century. Tofu is a basic food that is complicated to make. First, soy beans have to be boiled and processed before *nigari* (a mineral mix extracted from seawater) is added as a coagulant; then the clumpy curds are pressed in a wooden block, removing much of the liquid. It's hard to imagine how someone figured out the steps it takes to make tofu from soy beans.

When the Buddhist monks introduced tofu to Japan, they called it "Chinese curds." Eventually, the Chinese word, which is today *doufu*, was borrowed into Japanese and then into English as "tofu." This linguistic process happened a lot—see the section on ramen later in this book. Tofu caught on, especially because it's healthy and full of nutrients, which allowed it to replace meat in diets.

Like rice, tofu was initially considered a luxury item and eaten by the elites in the shogunate of the Edo period. Farmers were allowed to make and eat tofu only on special holidays. By the middle of the Tokugawa Shogunate, though, tofu was allowed to be eaten by everyone regardless of status. Matthew C. Perry took soy beans home after he opened Japan to trade with America, and today, the descendants of those beans are part of the annual US

crop that's exported to Japan. According to the Japan Tofu Association, the country consumes 4.9 million tons of tofu every year,
but only grows a small fraction of its own soy beans. Japan imports
ninety percent of its soy from the US!

✳

My mom used to make her own tofu at home. When our family
moved to the States in the mid-sixties, products like tofu weren't
available in a typical suburban grocery store or supermarket chain.
We drove from northern Virginia into Washington, DC, every
weekend so she could stock up on Japanese goods, but she didn't
like the quality of the packaged tofu that was available there. So she
made a wooden box with holes drilled in the sides to allow water
to seep out, and a top that could be weighed down with a rock.
She soaked the soy beans overnight, mixed the beans in a blender,
boiled the slurry, and pressed the mixture into the boxes with the
nigari coagulant. *Voila*—tofu!

But wait, there's more. Soy is an amazing food because all of it
is usable. For instance, when the beans are boiled and before the
nigari is added, a filmy skin forms on top of the liquid. That can
be skimmed off and dried into *yuba*, tofu skin, which is used in
many dishes, including deep-fried and wrinkly, tan *aburaage* sacks,
used to top off bowls of udon or filled with seasoned rice for *inari*
sushi. My mom always used another byproduct of her tofu making,
okara, the dregs of the beans after boiling. My mom would collect it
when she made tofu and pan-fry it with finely chopped vegetables,
shrimp, scallops, aburaage, soy sauce, sugar, and sake to make *unohana*, a tasty and healthy side dish. We later found out tofu manufacturers threw out or gave their okara to be used in animal feed,

and got bags for free from a company called Denver Tofu before it went out of business. And of course, the beans can be mashed and fermented to make soy sauce and miso paste.

Although Japanese restaurants throughout the US by the 1960s used tofu and served miso soup, they were often careful to use terms that didn't seem too mysterious to Americans, like calling tofu "bean curd" in a *New York Times* article as late as 1974, or they simply used a Japanese word on the assumption that their diners were Japanese or sophisticated enough to understand that "*Aka-dashi*" was a type of miso soup (from a 1953 menu for Imperial Gardens restaurant in Los Angeles).

The most familiar of all Japanese food exports for over a hundred years, even before Japanese food became popular in the United States, has been soy sauce, or *shoyu* in Japanese. It's a condiment that I bet most, if not all, Americans have had at one time or other. Its salty, pleasing umami flavor profile makes food taste better, whether it's added to meat or fish or sweetened as teriyaki sauce.

The plot of its origins is similar to other imports. Zen Buddhist monks brought back a version of what would become soy sauce from China, a salty fermented soy bean paste. It was a cross between today's soy sauce and miso paste, and the Japanese called it *hishio*. During the fermenting of hishio in the thirteenth century, a man teaching the process to villagers in Yuasa saw a deep-brown liquid seeping out of the barrel and tasted it. Soy sauce!

During the Edo period's years of isolation, when trade with the Dutch and Chinese from the port of Nagasaki was the only export and import option available, locally brewed soy sauce from Kyushu

"Vintage-Flavor"

KIKKOMAN
SOY SAUCE

Kikkoman adds the "Flavor-Touch" that means so much in everyday foods such as hamburger, chicken, steaks and chops, fish, etc., as well as for barbecuing and oriental dishes. Kikkoman is the winner of 30 major international awards for distinguished quality and flavor.

BASIC
for good
cooking

so **superior** *it's sensational!*

Good Housekeeping

AT LEADING MARKETS

THE VARIETIES OF SOY: (*top left*) A vintage ad for "Vintage-Flavor" Kikkoman *shoyu*. It even came with the Good Housekeeping seal of approval! (*bottom left*) Fresh tofu served at Toufuya Ukai in Tokyo. What better way to enjoy quality tofu than straight up?

PERRY'S BLACK SHIPS: (*above*) A lithograph depicting Commodore Matthew Perry's arrival at Yokohama, a pivotal moment for the country, not to mention its cuisine.

and western Honshu made its way to China, southeast Asia, and to parts of Europe. So when Commodore Perry's navy ships took soy beans back to America, its immediate purpose was to make soy sauce. Tofu came much later.

The best-known brand of soy sauce today is Kikkoman, although in the US, especially before World War II, soy sauce was considered only a Chinese ingredient. Kikkoman has its roots in Noda, a town in Chiba Prefecture east of Tokyo, which became the hub for soy-sauce brewing in the Kanto region during the late Edo period and into the twentieth century. In 1917 three families that manufactured soy sauce in Noda formed an association, then merged into one company, the Noda Shoyu Corporation, selling Kikkoman soy sauce. By the post–World War II years, Kikkoman was sold in the distinctive, curvy tabletop bottle with the bright-red plastic pouring top. In more recent years, the company added a lower-sodium version with a green top. Kikkoman saw the potential of the American market and opened a sales office in San Francisco in 1957 and a plant in Wisconsin to produce soy sauce in 1973.

Because of the company's very early entry into the American market (the only competition in the US at the time was La Choy, a company selling canned Chinese foods), Kikkoman was savvy with its marketing efforts. They advertised in mainstream American magazines with images of white families at a backyard grill, urging readers to try Kikkoman soy sauce to enhance the flavor of meats and seafood. They often offered recipes to introduce their products, including a premixed teriyaki sauce (anathema to a cook in Japan). One ad for Kikkoman soy sauce in a *Nisei Favorites* cookbook from the early sixties proclaims, "Kikkoman adds the 'flavor-touch' that means so much in everyday foods such as hamburger, chicken, steaks and chops, fish, etc. as well as for barbecuing and oriental dishes." Note that "oriental" mentioned at the end is the only reference to Asian, much less Japanese, cuisine.

Kikkoman's marketing efforts—and the quality of its US-brewed shoyu—helped push the brand past its established competitors, La Choy and Chun King, by the 1970s.

Today, gluten-free soy sauce is available in the form of *tamari*, which doesn't use any wheat. Typical soy sauces are brewed with both soy beans and wheat, which means people who are gluten intolerant or have Celiac disease, need to avoid it. Tamari is ironically full-circle for soy sauce, because it's most like the original soy sauce captured from that barrel of hishio in the thirteenth century. Kikkoman today sells tamari along with a line of soups and sauces to complement its main soy sauce.

In Japanese households, it's rude to pour plain soy sauce over rice, but I did it all the time to add that umami kick to plain rice, risking a yell and a swat from my mom.

"The essence of flavor": MSG

There's one more Japanese food staple worth mentioning, although it's not as popular today as it was just a few decades ago: MSG, under its best-known brand name, Ajinomoto.

Although it's associated with "Chinese restaurant syndrome," the controversy over monosodium glutamate (MSG) is actually one that began in Japan and with Japanese food. MSG is a naturally occurring chemical in *konbu*, a kind of seaweed (it's also naturally present in tomatoes and cheese) that's used as a base ingredient in lots of soups and sauces because it imparts a savory flavor.

A Japanese biochemist, Kikunae Ikeda, identified glutamic acid in konbu in 1908 and in 1909 created a way to manufacture it as monosodium glutamate. He coined the term umami, which is now a commonly accepted fifth basic flavor profile in food science, in addition to salty, sweet, bitter, and sour.

I grew up with MSG under the brand name Ajinomoto (the literal translation is "flavor thing," or more poetically, "essence of flavor"), the company that Ikeda formed to manufacture MSG for consumers. Ajinomoto was so commonly used by my mom that I once sprinkled it on breakfast cereal and promptly spit it out all over the table. MSG did not enhance the flavor of Cheerios.

As I grew up, the use of MSG in general as well as in my mom's kitchen declined, though it was widely used in Asian cooking, including Japanese and Chinese restaurants. I never had it around in college.

I was unaware that criticism at the time was building up against MSG, thanks to a 1968 letter by a Chinese doctor who had emigrated to America several years earlier, which was published in the *New England Journal of Medicine.* He noted mysterious symptoms he felt after eating at Chinese restaurants in the US, which included palpitations, numbness, and weakness. The letter ran with the headline "Chinese-Restaurant Syndrome," and the name—and the reputation—stuck.

In the healthy-food fad decades since, MSG took a bad rap. Many restaurants no longer use it to enhance the flavor of their dishes. In fact, restaurants proudly post signs proclaiming "No MSG!" But an increasing number of scientists and chefs have come out in recent years to defend MSG (not surprisingly, so has Ajinomoto's public relations department) and insist that MSG is safe and that the general public's call to ban the product is actually racist and anti-Asian. Celebrity chef David Chang has been one of the most vocal defenders of MSG in editorials, YouTube videos, and TED Talks. Even the US Food and Drug Administration has determined that MSG is safe, though it does note that some people can have reactions to it.

I've often thought in the past that after eating food with MSG, I feel a sort of a weird "high" and sometimes a spacey dizziness. But maybe that's just the power of (negative) suggestion. After all, MSG is a naturally occurring chemical in lots of foods and is present in all sorts of packaged food that I eat. A lot. Like nacho cheese Doritos, just as a glaring example. I don't feel a buzz after pigging out on chips.

It's odd that Japanese restaurants were spared the direct controversy of MSG and the "Chinese restaurant syndrome," but Japanese cookbooks seem to reflect the anti-MSG controversy. In a 1966 cookbook of *Nisei Favorites* by the Gardena Valley Baptist Church, for instance, many recipes list "Ajinomoto" by brand as an ingredient. By 1975, the Saint Louis Chapter Japanese American Citizens League's *Nisei Kitchen* cookbook lists the ingredient by its controversial chemical name, MSG, but does include it in some recipes (in sushi rice, for instance). The Saint Louis JACL still reprints and sells this cookbook.

Whether people today avoid MSG or embrace it, umami, the original word coined by biochemist Kikunae Ikeda way back in 1908, is now commonplace with chefs, critics, and foodies everywhere.

Chinese food may have taken the blame for the MSG controversy because, by the 1960s, it was by far the best-known Asian food in the United States. Even recently, as former *New York Times* writer Jennifer 8. Lee stated in her excellent history of American Chinese food (as opposed to authentic Chinese food), *Fortune Cookie Chronicles*, there are more Chinese restaurants in the US than McDonald's, Burger King, and Wendy's combined, making Chinese food as American as apple pie.

First Course

The "Big Three" of Japanese Food in America

On June 28, 1963, the number-one song on the American *Billboard* charts was "Ue O Muite Arukou," which translates to "I Look Up as I Walk." It's a plaintive lament by the Japanese pop star Kyu Sakamoto—known as the Elvis of Japan because he was a handsome singer and movie star. Its chorus goes, "I look up as I walk so that my tears won't fall."

While it sat at the top of the US charts, it was not called "Ue O Muite Arukou," admittedly a title that would have been difficult for most non-Japanese to say. The song was instead called "Sukiyaki." Mind you, it has nothing to do with sukiyaki the Japanese dish. It was simply chosen as the title in the West to accommodate English speakers. The tactic worked—the song, which sat atop the top pop lists for three weeks, had already been a huge hit in Japan under its original title in 1961, and spent three *months* at the top of the

Japanese bestseller chart. It was voted the number-one song of the year in Japan. It's been covered a number of times, with the best-known version by the R&B group Taste of Honey in 1980 (with new English words written to fit the melody).

Given the sadness of the lyrics and emotion in Sakamoto's singing, the song should have been called by another Japanese word that most Westerners, including Americans, would have known in 1963, "Sayonara." That's a more apt title, and one that most English speakers would have been able to remember and say, partly because of the 1957 film starring Marlon Brando as an American pilot during the Korean War who falls in love with a woman while he's stationed in Japan.

But the word "Sukiyaki" was chosen by a British music producer who was traveling in Japan in 1962 and heard Sakamoto's version. When he returned to England, he arranged for a group, Kenny Ball and the Jazzmen, to record an instrumental version of the catchy melody with his new title. The song made it to the top ten of the British music charts (it would have been difficult to bump off the Beatles, who were just starting their worldwide chart run), and as luck would have it, the track crossed the Atlantic. A radio disc jockey in Seattle, Washington, heard the instrumental version with the foodie title and began playing it. It didn't take long for Capitol Records (ironically, the label the Beatles would release their hits on) to seek out the original Japanese version, slap the British title on the single, and put it out into the world. It remains to this day the only Japanese song to top the charts in the United States, and until the Korean boy band BTS in 2020, the only Asian act to top the American charts.

Two interesting facts to note about the song and its title: The British producer chose "Sukiyaki" for the track's title because when he was traveling in Japan he enjoyed the dish sukiyaki. And, although the song fits the oeuvre of sad love songs about a man looking back at a lost love, then looking forward with hope for happiness beyond the clouds, it was actually a protest song.

The song was written by lyricist Rokusuke Ei and composer Hachidai Nakamura. Ei said at the time that he wrote the lyrics on his way home from a failed protest, and his frustrations spilled over so he had to walk looking up to keep from crying. What was he protesting? The continued presence of American troops in Japan since the end of World War II.

Up to an estimated thirty million Japanese—a third of the population at the time—demonstrated against the security treaty signed between the US and Japan in 1960, allowing the US to establish military bases throughout the country (today, most of them are based on Okinawa). But the protests failed, and Japan's parliament ratified the treaty the year that Ei wrote "Sukiyaki." The song crystallized the mourning of the people who fought against the treaty, and yet it embodied an upbeat, optimistic spirit in its melody and arrangement.

And the title that was tacked onto the song perfectly crystallized Americans' awareness of Japanese food at the time.

Sukiyaki

Thanks to the returning GIs after World War II, some with Japanese "war brides" despite the racism they would most likely face, many Americans came to know a thing or two about Japan. The men and women coming back from Japan brought bits of culture in ceramics, tea sets, lacquerware, dolls, hanging scrolls, and screens, and they brought back an appreciation of some Japanese food. "Some" is the operative word. For one thing, Japan was still devastated in the immediate postwar years, and many people lived in poverty, relying on the black market. And for another, the major cities' restaurant culture that we applaud today would take time to become re-established.

The typical GIs that served in the Occupation years didn't necessarily dine out on sushi and sashimi—that likely would have been too exotic or unavailable. General Douglas MacArthur, Supreme Commander for the Allied Powers, may have been able to stay at the Hotel New Grand in Yokohama upon his arrival in Japan in 1945 and enjoy its *haute cuisine*, but even that was a pale improvisation in the early weeks after Japan's surrender. The hotel served MacArthur and his military retinue an Army specialty—spaghetti made with ketchup for sauce. The New Grand may have gussied it up for the general with meat and tomato sauce in addition to the ketchup, but the dish was brought to Japan by the US military, and it's on the menu to this day.

The rank-and-file soldiers would only eat more typical fare, street food like ramen, or they stuck to their canned rations and Spam (which caught on and became hugely popular in Okinawa).

They brought back the souvenirs, artwork, cameras, and Hi-Fi stereo equipment at exchange rates that made everything bought in Japan very affordable. The exchange rate was held at ¥360 to the dollar from the end of the war until 1971, and that made shopping in Japan, and especially in the military PX (post exchange) stores, incredibly inexpensive.

The returning Americans also brought back a familiarity with three Japanese dishes: sukiyaki, teriyaki, and tempura. These three were the main types of Japanese food that most Americans were familiar with, unless you were a Japanese immigrant, had traveled to Japan before the war, or were an adventurous soldier during the Occupation.

Still, the three were a good representation of the basic flavor palette in Japan.

The simplest description of sukiyaki, which comes up often in descriptions of the song title for Kyu Sakamoto's hit, is that it's a Japanese "hotpot" dish. It is a hotpot dish in that it's all cooked in one pot. In Japan, a dish cooked in a single pot would be described as *nabemono*, but sukiyaki is usually cooked not in a deep saucepan or stockpot but in a skillet. My dad used an ancient, square-shaped electric skillet that had an old-school thick electric cord wrapped in black fabric, with metallic thread woven through it. It was placed in the center of the table where we'd drop vegetables and meat into the skillet, which was about four inches deep, enough to accommodate a shallow layer of sweet and savory dashi, and let them cook together, then serve the mixture communal-style.

Today, when my wife and I and her family cook sukiyaki, it's a bigger affair, with two large, round modern electric skillets to cook up the sukiyaki fixings. The basic ingredients include thin-sliced beef, tofu, napa cabbage, *shirataki* noodles or pieces of *konnyaku* (jellied mountain yams), *kamaboko* (fish cakes), mushrooms (*matsutake* if available), *shungiku* (chrysanthemum greens), and green onions. There are no hard-and-fast rules on what you can drop into the broth, so there are seafood sukiyaki, vegetarian variations, and so on. In many cases, a raw egg is beaten in a small bowl and the food is dipped in it before eating.

In Osaka, the meat is grilled separately and then the vegetables are added. Finally, the broth is poured on top. Sukiyaki might be considered a middle-class comfort food by some, but it can be luxurious. One year, my uncle and aunt in Sapporo took us out to a high-end sukiyaki restaurant that was famous for its quality of ingredients and service. After we'd finished the ingredients, the server in kimono entered our room and added soba noodles into the leftover broth so that we wouldn't have to waste anything.

The key ingredient for sukiyaki is the broth, which is most often a simple combination of water (or dashi), soy sauce, sake, and mirin (a sweet, lower-alcohol version of sake).

Sukiyaki has a long history in Japan. Its origin story is that farmers used their spades, or *suki*, to grill, or *yaki*, their meat and vegetables together. The image of someone holding a spade over a fire to cook food seems weird and awkward to me, so it's just as well that electric skillets were invented for this purpose.

The oldest sukiyaki restaurant in Tokyo, Iseju, has been serving the dish since 1869, so it's definitely a defining dish and a traditional favorite in Japan.

Sukiyaki is a sister dish to *shabu-shabu*, another one-pot meal. For shabu-shabu, water, lightly flavored with a piece of konbu seaweed—not the sweet, more flavorful broth of sukiyaki—is heated over a burner or electric skillet and, when boiling, vegetables are added; then each diner dips thinly sliced meat into the pot and swishes it around until it's barely cooked. The name "shabu-shabu" is an onomatopoeic description of the swishing.

Although there isn't a very good Western comparison for sukiyaki or shabu-shabu—both meals are communal in nature, with the food cooked with the diners around the table—maybe shabu-shabu is sort of like fondue, without the cheese. Once cooked, the ingredients are dipped in either a soy *ponzu* or sesame-based *tsuyu* sauce.

Teriyaki

As Japanese food became accepted in the United States, it helped to have a number-one pop song named after one of its most familiar dishes. There hasn't been a song for teriyaki, but in the decades following World War II, teriyaki became the second of the triad of dishes that Americans came to enjoy. But, although the two sound similar, teriyaki is a little different from sukiyaki, because "teriyaki" doesn't describe the dish itself but rather the way the meat or fish is flavored. Teriyaki is the sauce, not the entree, and is most often used with fish, not other meats. In fact, the word "teriyaki" is rarely used to describe a dish in Japan, unless it's to identify a McDonald's teriyaki chicken burger or the Japanese fast-food chain MOS Burger's teriyaki burger, which was created because of how popular teriyaki had become in the US.

My mom had her own recipe for teriyaki sauce, which I

THE TRIUMVIRATE: (*top*) The first Japanese restaurant in Minneapolis, Tokyo Restaurant. Diners are greeted with "Sukiyaki" and "Tempura" in the front window. (*above*) On full display, the sukiyaki, teriyaki, tempura triumvirate, which were the order of the day. From Imperial Garden's 1953 menu.

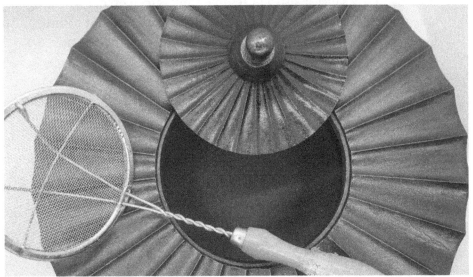

MAKING TEMPURA AT HOME: (*top*) My mom making *kakiage* at home. This is a kind of tempura with bits of vegetables and seafood fried together in a light batter. (*above*) A heavy pot made of cast iron used to fry tempura. This one used to be my mother's.

bastardized by using beer instead of sake and mirin when I went off to college. It never occurred to me to use it for burgers, though.

Teriyaki, like many Japanese dishes, has a lot of room for customization and personalization. That's how the sauce could be used in a whole new way in America, then come back and be adapted for Japan. I don't follow my mom's recipe for teriyaki sauce anymore. I've learned to make it with half the sugar and to substitute low-sodium soy sauce (and now, gluten-free tamari) for the original Kikkoman shoyu. I no longer have beer around (I'm allergic to alcohol, I learned after college) but I do have cheap sake for cooking. Once the ingredients are combined, the sauce is heated and reduced to taste. Thicker sauce is ideal for brushing onto meat or fish as it cooks or drizzling over when it's served. Thinner is better for marinating. Bottled teriyaki sauce is available, but it seems silly to buy it premade when it's easy to throw the ingredients together starting from plain soy sauce. I also add sesame seeds, green onions, garlic, and ginger to teriyaki and related marinades that I use for dishes like steak or chicken shish kebabs.

Teriyaki as a flavoring has been a staple of Japanese cooking since the seventeenth century, but it was mostly used for fish well into the twentieth century. I've mentioned that beef was not commonly cooked until the Meiji period, but chicken has always been a more familiar part of the Japanese diet. "Yakitori" is a familiar word, though Americans may not know that in Japan it describes chicken pieces (all parts of a chicken, including breast, thigh, liver, and even heart) on a skewer, dipped in a teriyaki-like tsuyu and grilled over charcoal. Restaurants throughout Japan specialize in just yakitori.

You might notice a pattern with a lot of Japanese dishes—the suffix "yaki" (or in the case of "yakitori," prefix). "Yaki" simply means to grill or broil—basically, to cook. The first part of the word adds the specifics. Sukiyaki was food grilled on a spade; teriyaki is food that has a lustrous glaze on it (*"teri"*) after being grilled. The shine comes from the sugar in the marinade. In the case of yakitori, *"tori"* means bird, specifically chicken.

Chicken became a common food for the masses in Japan in the late 1800s—in ancient history they seemed to be more for pets and fighting than dining on—but oddly, teriyaki chicken wasn't popular in Japan until recent decades. In another cross-cultural twist, teriyaki chicken was an export from the United States to Japan. When Kikkoman opened its first sales office in the US in 1957, the company was looking for a way to make their products popular outside of Japanese food enthusiasts. To break into the "brand awareness" of mainstream (non-Japanese) Americans, Kikkoman came up with a brilliant marketing campaign.

A late-fifties ad for Kikkoman soy sauce shows a Caucasian mother and daughter beaming over dishes, with the title reading, "Recipes—Japanese American Cookery," and the tagline, "Tested, easy-to-do recipes to bring wonderful new variety to your menus." Adding the "American" to "Japanese American Cookery" demystified the use of soy sauce and made it safe for mainstream consumption.

By the sixties, summertime grilling on backyard barbecues was a symbol of the culinary American dream (along with diners serving milkshakes and early fast-food hamburger joints). So Kikkoman suggested that teriyaki chicken made with the company's bottled teriyaki sauce would be a terrific new taste sensation on a grill.

Even during the seventies, as shown by a 1973 magazine ad featuring delicious-looking meats right off a grill, Kikkoman included easy recipes for teriyaki spareribs, steaks, and chicken. "Easy does it—deliciously—when you discover Kikkoman Teriyaki: The sauce of great ideas," proclaimed the ad. "Simply use this superb combination of the world's finest soy sauce, choice wine and natural herbs and spices as a marinade, a baste and directly on foods as a seasoning. Try the tasty recipes below. You'll enjoy a revelation in flavor!"

That revelation led to the popularity of teriyaki chicken throughout America, though teriyaki chicken is a rare item on menus in Japan. For people in Japan, teriyaki is a *part* of cooking, not the final chicken, fish, or beef dish. In the US, teriyaki chicken is standard on every Japanese restaurant's menu, and Buddhist temples, Christian churches, and Japanese American community groups have been grilling up tens of thousands of pounds of teriyaki chicken for Cherry Blossom Festivals and other celebrations for over sixty years.

Teriyaki also has strong roots in Japanese Hawaiian culture, where immigrants in the Aloha State made a marinade of soy sauce with pineapples, which added both sweetness and a way to tenderize meats. So Hawaiian-style teriyaki has a tropical flavor that makes it distinct from mainland teriyaki.

But teriyaki has yet another regional distinction.

If pizza is part of New York City's identity (sorry, Chicago) and cheesesteak sandwiches belong to Philadelphia, teriyaki evokes Seattle. Toshi Kasahara, a Japanese immigrant who went to college in Portland, Oregon, and settled in Seattle, Washington, opened an eponymous restaurant, Toshi's Teriyaki Restaurant, near the city's famous futuristic Space Needle in 1976. He served a simple menu of grilled teriyaki chicken or thin-sliced beef, or steak, and, for a change-up, chicken curry, all served with a mound of rice and shredded cabbage salad. The teriyaki chicken plate at the time sold for all of $1.85. Today it runs $9.50, still not outrageous.

The success of his restaurant and a second location spawned over a hundred teriyaki shops around Seattle, and non-Japanese restaurants including Vietnamese, Chinese, and even an Ethiopian restaurant serve their versions of "teriyaki chicken." For his part, Toshi now bottles and sells his teriyaki sauces, and the original location was featured on the Food Network's *Delicious Destinations* cable television series.

Tempura

While teriyaki has become more famous and common in the United States—okay, maybe more so in certain parts of the US—tempura, the third Japanese dish that became well-known in the postwar years, has been somewhat eclipsed in its glamour and ubiquity.

Tempura's origins are in the Portuguese merchants and Catholic missionaries who had arrived in Kyushu before the Edo period, in the sixteenth century. When the Edo period began, Tokugawa Ieyasu favored the Dutch to become the trading partners at the port of Nagasaki. But his favorite dish was the adapted Portuguese dish of batter-fried vegetables for *quatuor tempora*, the days of fasting where no meat was allowed—thus the name "tempura."

Tempura can be made at home. I still have a cast-iron tempura frying pan, with a collar to drain the freshly fried pieces plucked out of the oil, that my family used for special occasions. My mom also used to make *kakiage*, a tempura made with small chopped pieces of shrimp and vegetables mixed into a palm-sized serving and deep-fried. She would make a large batch and freeze them to eat whenever she wanted one. Or two. Or three.

Although tempura can be a homemade dish—and it's probably much more common in Japanese homes—I think of tempura primarily as a restaurant dish. Preparing the ingredients, dipping them in batter, and then frying them doesn't seem like a lot of work, but it can be a challenge of timing and tidiness. Anyone who's made fried chicken, or worse, a whole fried turkey (even without batter), can testify to the splatter all over the kitchen. So I prefer ordering tempura off a menu at a restaurant and letting them handle the mess.

In the postwar years, my mother-in-law's family settled in Denver. They rarely went out to restaurants, because, as my mother-in-law says, her *obaachan* (grandmother) believed that the family should eat food from the grocery store and cook at home. She remembers her mother, grandmother, and aunt cooking together in the kitchen. Her family made American and traditional Japanese dishes. But she never really liked the shrimp tempura very much, so she would hide the pieces in a storage space under the dining room table. When the family moved years later, dried up shrimp tempura tumbled out.

My wife's family also has a vivid memory from Akebono, a longtime Denver restaurant that was started initially on Larimer Street and later moved across the street to Sakura Square, Denver's

"Tiny Tokyo" district built in 1972. Akebono opened during World War II in 1942 as Fred's Place, named after owner Fred Aoki, as a pool hall with a kitchen where his wife, Chiyoko Aoki, served up Japanese, Chinese, and American dishes. In 1961 the name was changed to Akebono.

Regular customers including my wife's family remember her tempura best, which featured a light and crispy batter that was almost like lace on the shrimp and vegetables. My wife, who ran around the restaurant and into the kitchen when she was young, recalls Mrs. Aoki dipping her hand into the batter and then flicking bits of batter onto the tempura as it was frying, leading to the unusually delicate and delicious end result. Her tempura was paired with the restaurant's most popular menu item, the Teri-Ten Combination, which paired the Aoki touch on tempura with thin-sliced teriyaki beef.

A typical order of tempura in any Japanese restaurant has been the same for decades, maybe for a hundred years. It includes a couple of pieces of large shrimp (artfully prepared with shallow cuts across the belly to keep them from curling), a curved slice of *kabocha* (Japanese pumpkin), onion, *renkon* (lotus root), carrots, perhaps green peppers, and. if the chef is artistic, fried *shiso* leaves. Like sukiyaki or shabu-shabu or many other Japanese dishes, the options are as varied as what's available in the kitchen. The trick is to get the batter right and have a light hand with the frying, so that the tempura isn't covered with a thick, bready coating. It's even worse if the batter doesn't cook all the way and it's still gooey inside.

✳

Since Americans know about panko, even if they can't pronounce it correctly, it should be noted that panko-coated fried dishes are not tempura. The frozen "panko shrimp" at Costco is not a substitute for frozen shrimp tempura, which Costco also sells. And the popular dish *tonkatsu*, breaded fried pork cutlet, which is dipped in batter like tempura then coated with panko, is also not a form of tempura.

Karaage, Japanese-style fried marinated chicken, almost fits the definition of tempura, but tempura isn't made with marinated ingredients. Diners dip tempura in the *tentsuyu* sauce for flavor, but karaage is cooked with the flavor already infused. It might seem like a fine distinction, but it's an important one. No one dips fried chicken into a sauce, unless it's a dab of flavored mayonnaise or you've bought chicken nuggets from a fast food joint that comes with several icky, gloppy dipping sauces. A restaurant will get all the details down, including the tentsuyu, which is made with the standby dashi soup base, soy sauce, mirin, and sugar. It's best when grated daikon radish, called *daikon oroshi*, is added.

Searching the internet for tempura at Japanese restaurants in

Los Angeles leads to one shop on Wilshire Boulevard charging $18 for a shrimp and vegetable tempura lunch. That's probably typical for a fancy Japanese eatery today. A few yesterdays ago, in 1953, a few blocks away on Wilshire Boulevard, at the Imperial Gardens Sukiyaki restaurant, the "Tempura DeLuxe Dinner" with tempura shrimp, yakitori, *suimono* (clear soup), *sunomono* (cucumber salad), *tsukemono* (pickles), rice, green tea, and tea cakes for dessert put diners back $3.50.

To round out the early Japanese food triumvirate, in 1953 Imperial Gardens offered an equally robust "Sukiyaki DeLuxe Dinner" for $3.50 with beef or $4.00 with chicken alongside "Teriyaki Dinners": $3.95 for the yakitori, $3.50 for sliced top sirloin, a luxurious $5 for filet mignon, and a more down-to-earth $3.25 for teriyaki fish "Broiled in Soy Sauce," served with a side of tempura shrimp.

Wow, how times have changed!

If a Japanese pop song became a hit in the US today, it surely would be allowed to keep its Japanese title. But what if it were a long title with difficult Japanese words for Americans to pronounce? Would cultural sensitivity force Western listeners to get used to a title they couldn't say correctly? Or would some record company or radio executive give it a (hopefully culturally appropriate) English title?

That's a test of how much times and values have really changed. We'll just have to wait and see. After all, the Korean boy band BTS has become huge in the US by releasing hit singles in English.

Food, like pop music, adapts to changing tastes to reach a larger audience.

Entree

Over a Century of Japanese Restaurants

For most Americans, foreign or ethnic foods are introduced via restaurants. Food is the gateway to culture. As awareness of world cultures expands and globalization connects us all to not just products from around the globe but also to food, Americans have become exposed to a wider variety of cuisines. Some cultures even benefit from fads, both culinary and pop cultural—anime can be the first introduction for some young people today to Japanese food. With increasing exposure comes curiosity and, ultimately, more sophisticated tastes.

In Japan, food culture has become such an important part of society and the economy that the country is now renowned for some of the best dining in the world.

The Michelin Guide was introduced in 1900 to list restaurants (and auto repair shops) in France for drivers traveling the country.

The now-famous star system was added with a single star in 1926 to designate the best restaurants, and in 1931 the three-star system was cemented. In the 2020 version of the influential Michelin Guide, France has the most starred restaurants in the world with 628. The second country is Japan with 577 and Italy is third with 374. The United States comes in fifth with 169 Michelin-starred restaurants.

Among cities, Tokyo boasts the most starred restaurants in the world in the 2020 Michelin Guide with 226 entries (it's held the title for more than a decade, with Paris in second place).

Clearly, Japanese cuisine has arrived.

Restaurants serving Japanese cuisine to the West first opened almost one hundred and fifty years ago, on the heels of a faddish fascination with Japan and Japanese culture. After several hundred years of isolation, Japan had finally opened for business, and the young Meiji Emperor's reign was embracing the industry and culture of America and Europe. Western foods and cooking styles, like French cuisine, became a symbol of sophistication and class in Japan. Western restaurants sprouted up, too, mostly to serve the arriving foreigners in the international districts set up for them in Tokyo and other cities.

But the cultural exchange went both ways. Europeans and Americans gave in to curiosity about Japan—they knew something about Chinese culture and, certainly, India, thanks to the British Empire's colonial history. But Japan was new and mysterious and exotic.

In 1884, the Japanese government sponsored an exhibit in London with a demonstration of Japanese cuisine, sending a Japanese chef and staff to cook in what today might be called a "pop-up" restaurant called Nippon Ryoriya (literally, Japanese Cuisine Shop).

The meal was served with traditional lacquerware bowls and plates in a space that was decorated to look Japanese.

First performed in 1885, Gilbert and Sullivan's *The Mikado*, a comic opera set in the fictional village of Titipu (an outrageously stupid name that isn't remotely Japanese), was a racially stereotyped fantasy version of Japan. It was inspired in part by the fascination sweeping the continent for all things Japanese—an exhibition of a recreated Japanese village was due to open in England after it debuted. Across the English Channel, a group of rambunctious French painters had banded together, inspired in large part by the Japanese woodblock prints that had begun to appear in Europe (many were used as mere wrapping paper for gifts that were shipped from Japan) and the colors and spatial concepts of their images, to invent a movement that's now called Impressionism.

The first wave

Arts and culture weren't the only Japanese influence on the West. Early Japanese restaurants opened too, in England as well as in America. When *The Mikado* opened in New York City in August 1885, one historian noted that suddenly, "all things Japanese were the height of fashion." New York chef Louis Sherry, whose legacy today is best known for the premium chocolates and candies in fancy tins that bear his name, opened his first restaurant in New York City in the 1880s and was inspired by *The Mikado* to serve a menu that reflected Japanese elements—or what he thought of as Japanese—to his upper-crust diners. But like the opera itself, the "all things Japanese" may have been fantasies of what Japan was like, not a realistic image. In 1876, only ten Japanese lived in the city, and by the turn of the century, there were a thousand. There surely were Japanese restaurants serving the small immigrant community, but it wasn't like on the West Coast.

In Seattle, which had a concentration of Japanese immigrants much like San Francisco and Los Angeles to the south, there were Japanese restaurants available for diners of all races to partake. A Caucasian who had arrived in Seattle in 1888 to look for work with just a few dollars to his name noted in one journal that he was able to eat at a Japanese restaurant for fifteen cents.

A magazine article about San Francisco's restaurant scene noted that the author had heard there were Japanese restaurants in town. A *Los Angeles Times* article from 1896 proclaimed that the city's inexpensive Japanese restaurants were better than other eateries because of the staff: "The Japs are universally suave and polite." That didn't help eleven years later in 1907 when a mob in an anti-Japanese riot destroyed a Japanese restaurant and bathhouse in Los Angeles, according to *the New York Times*.

An article in the *Times* in 1903 about how the St. Nicholas Garden had been converted into a Japanese-style village, with kimono-clad "geishas" serving tea and fixing the hairdos and

"For Junior Prom"
. . . .
For junior prom, while most people went to Olive Garden, we made reservations at Bush Garden, a formal Japanese restaurant that had been open since 1960 in downtown Portland. Our Japanese teacher had introduced us to the restaurant by making it part of the annual Japanese class trip. Bush Garden was the first time most of us had been to a restaurant with tatami rooms, and the unique appeal of it made it perfect for a gaggle of outcast high school students wanting to make their prom dinner stand out from everyone else's.

Cay Fletcher

manicures of visiting ladies, mentions that a Japanese restaurant is included as a part of the attraction.

One corner property in Los Angeles' Boyle Heights neighborhood, which is just a few minutes east from the Japanese American National Museum, began life in the 1920s as a grocery store. Like many Japanese- or Japanese American–owned businesses, the property was shut during World War II as the owners were sent to concentration camps. After the war, the building housed a Japanese American barber shop, florist, and grocery store. Otemo Sushi Cafe opened in 1956. It's since been renamed Otomisan Japanese Restaurant—the last Japanese restaurant in Boyle Heights and one of the oldest continuously operating Japanese restaurants in Los Angeles. In 2020, the property including the restaurant was submitted as a Historic-Cultural Monument by the Los Angeles Conservancy in partnership with the Boyle Heights Community Partners.

Another longtime Los Angeles Japanese restaurant was Imperial Gardens Sukiyaki, which was located on Wilshire Boulevard in the 1950s until moving to Sunset Boulevard, becoming a haven for Hollywood celebrities by the 1970s. The restaurant clearly reflected the sukiyaki-teriyaki-tempura triumvirate in its early years.

Back up the West Coast, in Seattle, a Japanese restaurant named Maneki has been operating since 1904—an incredible track record—with a break during World War II, when its owners were incarcerated. After the war, the original building in the Nihonmachi (Japantown) section of what is today part of the Chinatown International District was looted and damaged, so Maneki reopened in its nearby current location. The restaurant has the distinction of being not only the oldest Japanese restaurant in Seattle, but also the first sushi bar in the city.

*

Japanese food probably wouldn't have caught on if Chinese food hadn't paved the way as the first Asian cuisine to make its way across the Pacific. By the early twentieth century, Americans were already chowing down ("chow" is a word originally from Chinese Pidgin English) on food cooked by Chinese using non-traditional ingredients available in the US, like chop suey (basically a mashup of leftovers or whatever ingredients are available). In fact, early Japanese restaurants appealed to white customers by making sure to serve chop suey on their menus. That's why the Cherry Blossom Restaurant in Los Angeles, which opened in the 1930s, prominently featured signs proclaiming to offer chop suey, chow mein, fried rice, and "Egg Foyeoung" on its menu, not to mention the "short order" items like rib steak, ham and eggs, and bacon and eggs. Japanese restaurants had many additional attractions, like Fred's Place mentioned in the previous chapter, which started life as a pool hall, cooking up Chinese, American, and Japanese items on its menu.

That's in contrast to today, when non-Japanese Asians can benefit from the popularity of Japanese restaurants in America. A 2016 Washington Post article explained "Why so many of America's sushi restaurants are owned by Chinese immigrants": Japanese food makes more economic sense because it's popular today and generally more expensive than Chinese food, offering a higher profit margin. Also there are so many Chinese restaurants and takeout shops in the country that the competition keeps prices low. At the time of the article, Japan's Ministry of Agriculture estimated only about ten percent of Japanese restaurants in the US were run by Japanese.

The Second Wave

Japanese restaurants existed before the war, but they grew in number in the postwar decades. In the early 1960s, when "Suki-yaki" topped the pop charts and sukiyaki, teriyaki, and tempura were still the main Japanese dishes known to Americans, Japan as a country and a culture was going through a general reinvention. The 1964 Olympics were held in Tokyo, and it was Japan's opportunity to re-emerge on the world stage and show off its recovery from the devastation of World War II, with not just a stable democratic government in place but the most modern technology and conveniences.

The Shinkansen, Japan's bullet train, made its debut just in time for the 1964 Olympics that October. My dad took our family on a train ride from Tokyo to Osaka and back so we could say we had ridden on the coolest, fastest train in the world.

In 1966, I watched footage of the Beatles on the small, flickering black-and-white television my dad bought, performing at the Budokan concert hall (yes, the same hall where Cheap Trick recorded a best-selling live album in 1977). Japanese electronics were being hailed as the best in the world, and so were their cameras. High-fidelity audio equipment, like radio receivers, record players, and reel-to-reel tape recorders, were much-sought purchases, especially by US military personnel during their tour of duty in Japan. Even though the Occupation was long over, US military were a common sight throughout Japan because of the Vietnam War. Panasonic was still called National then, but Sony was becoming a well-known international brand. Even the big Japanese automakers were on the verge of an international breakthrough, and within a decade cars by Toyota, Datsun (Nissan today), and

Mazda would appear on American roads and highways. Even after my family moved to the States, I carefully studied the PX catalogs for camera equipment that I wanted as a budding middle school and high school photographer in the seventies.

The rise of Japanese goods, culture, and cuisine was a slow but inexorable process that began after the war and accelerated for decades until Japanese food, as one measure, became mainstream and commonplace from the nineties and into the current day.

One of the reasons that Japanese food caught on in America starting in the sixties, and much more widely in the seventies and eighties, was the interest in "health food" and healthier lifestyles. During the seventies, jogging became all the rage, and in the post-sixties, post-hippie daze, "groovy" turned into granola and vegetarianism. Along with dropping meat, tofu became cool. So did bean sprouts, multigrain bread, kombucha, and yogurt. Gluten-free baked goods and tamari are a modern reflection of the same health-oriented lifestyle.

A 2013 report by the Japan External Trade Organization (JETRO) showed that outside of Japan almost eighty-four percent of people who were asked to name their favorite food answered Japanese. The top reason given for the choice was the flavor and the second reason was the perceived healthiness of Japanese cuisine.

The JETRO report cites a 1977 US Senate recommendation titled "Dietary Goals for the United States," which was also called the "McGovern Report," as one of the causes for the increasing interest in Japanese cuisine. "The report recommended that people consume carbohydrates (starchy material) in the form of

CHINESE AMERICANS PAVED THE WAY: (*top*) The famous "Chop Suey" sign in LA's Little Tokyo. A metaphor for the relationship between Chinese American and Japanese American foods. (*left*) If it weren't for the ubiquity of Chinese food in America, Japanese food and many other Asian immigrant cuisines might not have achieved mainstream success—not just on the coasts, but across America. Pictured here: the Silver Dragon restaurant in Coeur d'Alene, Idaho.

A CENTURY OF JAPANESE RESTAU-
RANT HISTORY: (*top*) Denver's very
own Akebono, originally named
Fred's Place, seen here in its original capacity as pool hall in addition
to restaurant. (*right*) The facade of
Otomisan Japanese Restaurant in
Los Angeles, one of the oldest continuously operated Japanese restaurants in the city and a monument
to the history of Japanese cuisine in
America.

"It Looked Like Snowflakes"

. . . .

My earliest Japanese restaurant memory is eating at Akebono in Denver and ordering Mrs. Aoki's beautiful shrimp tempura. . . . It looked like snowflakes and was too pretty to eat. They also made the best cabbage *tsukemono*, which I couldn't get enough of.

Erin Yoshimura

unrefined grains as a dietary staple, together with seasonal vegetables, seaweed, fish, and shellfish, while reducing intake of foods high in animal fats, sugar, and salt. This is exactly what traditional Japanese food is," JETRO proudly pointed out. (Never mind that many Japanese dishes are replete with salty and sweet ingredients!)

In the late seventies and into the eighties, sushi was becoming more prevalent on Japanese menus in America, especially around Los Angeles and other West Coast cities. The hipsters of the time, who included Hollywood celebrities of the day, considered sushi both "healthy" and "fashionable foreign food."

The JETRO report went on to state that the popularity of Japanese food in other countries, including the United States, spread in stages beginning with "pioneers" (the early adopters who explored sushi as a healthy food alternative) to the "development" period, when Japanese became a familiar genre in local restaurant scenes, with prices and dishes that were more accessible to everyday diners instead of just the privileged class. In the current, "realistic" period, diners are now seeking authentic and specialized Japanese food experiences, from eateries that only serve ramen or sushi, for instance, or serve it in distinctly Japanese formats, like *kaiseki*, the multi-course traditional meal of local, regional, and seasonal dishes served in leisurely fashion and immaculately presented.

Benihana

Foodies and fans of Japanese culture seem taken aback when I mention I want to include Benihana in this book. It's not real Japanese, they say, and it trivialized the food by turning it into entertainment by the chef cooking at the tabletop *teppanyaki* grill. Sure, it isn't traditional Japanese like kaiseki cuisine, and Benihana certainly did add an element of entertainment to dining out. But I think it's an important part of the journey of Japanese food in America. Here's why.

First, as I've already written, beef wasn't historically a mainstay of Japanese cuisine because of Buddhist dietary restrictions until the Meiji period, in the late 1800s. It's remarkable that Wagyu, top-quality Japanese beef with the spectacular marbling of fat and tender, flavorful, melt-in-your mouth meat, has become known across the world in such a short amount of time. After all, the Japanese Wagyu industry really only got its start after the country relaxed some of its trade restrictions just thirty years ago.

The literal translation of "Wagyu" is simply "Japanese cow," and the most common breed of cattle that's raised for Wagyu is Kuroge Washu. The industry is tightly regulated in Japan, with industry oversight that labels the best Wagyu as A5 (the highest grade), A4, and so on. There are a handful of regions that raise the much-coveted cows that can claim the top Wagyu ranking. Many people know the name "Kobe beef" because it's been aggressively marketed, but Kobe is just one of the cities that produce A5 Wagyu. Matsusaka, Hida, and Omi are a few other regions in Japan that are known for Wagyu beef. Increasingly, Wagyu is also grown and certified in other countries, including the United States.

Wagyu has become "mainstream" in spite of its high cost, and even big-box stores like Costco sometimes sell A5-certified Wagyu imported from Japan. But with food fads come imitators and knockoffs, and it's worth noting that if you see "Wagyu" without its heart attack–inducing price, beware. It's probably not Wagyu at all, but a premium cut of American beef, maybe Angus or a hybrid of Angus and Wagyu.

But long before the current fad over Wagyu, one restaurant brought the magic of Japanese beef cuisine to America ... albeit not exactly traditional Japanese cuisine.

Benihana of Tokyo was a stroke of marketing genius by its creator, Hiroaki "Rocky" Aoki, but it had true and authentic Japanese roots, even if those roots didn't dig deep into Japanese tradition. That's because the restaurant chain was a postwar invention.

First, the teppanyaki (a steel tabletop grill) is an adaptation of a flat griddle created after World War II in order to cook steaks for homesick American GIs during the Occupation, made famous at a Tokyo restaurant called Misono. Today, restaurants in Japan that advertise teppanyaki are filled more with foreign tourists than locals. In the US, most fans of Benihana and similar restaurants mistakenly call the teppanyaki grill a *hibachi*, which is an entirely different charcoal grill.

And second, the name Benihana was chosen by Aoki's father, Yunosuke Aoki, who had run a jazz cafe in the Nihonbashi district of Tokyo before the war. When coffee became hard to find during the war, he opened a shop next door and sold a sweet red bean soup called *oshiruko*. The neighborhood unfortunately was destroyed by American firebombing before the end of the war.

His wife, Katsu, saw a *benihana*—red flower—walking through a devastated Tokyo at the end of the war, and the couple used the name for a new coffee shop they opened.

The coffee shop was successful, and he expanded the business to a full-service restaurant in 1950. In 1955, he opened a barbecue restaurant across the street from his original location, and in 1962 he changed the name to Benihana Bekken and added a teppanyaki grill. He then opened a second location in the posh shopping district of Ginza.

So the teppanyaki idea was already in place when Aoki's son Rocky, an athlete who qualified to wrestle in the 1960 Rome Olympic games, decided to study business in America with the dream of opening a teppanyaki restaurant in New York City.

That's exactly what the younger Aoki did. He opened his Benihana of Tokyo restaurant in midtown Manhattan in 1964, the same year the Beatles invaded the US and, of course, the year the Olympics were held in Tokyo, heralding the re-emergence of Japan onto the world stage.

Japanese stuff was enjoying a new wave of faddish appreciation. And Aoki's brilliant idea of making Japanese cooking America-friendly was a hit ... though it needed a boost from a rave review in the *New York Herald Tribune* to get over the hump. Aoki purposely wanted to introduce Americans to Japanese food, but not too much Japanese food. Although Benihana restaurants now have sushi bars and serve a variety of "authentic" Japanese dishes, including sashimi, *gyoza* (or potstickers, which are yoshoku, originally from China), and tempura, back then he declared that the restaurant would not serve anything slimy or fishy—in other words, anything too Japanese. He stuck to four main proteins: beef, chicken, shrimp, and fish. Also included was a salad with a ginger-citrus-soy sauce dressing, fried rice, some veggies such as onion (which are stacked into a peak that spits flames like an "onion volcano"), and soup, back then a clear but savory soup, but these days also miso soup.

The chefs were initially all trained in Japan (or so they said) and performed in front of diners at the teppanyaki grill, tossing eggs in their chefs' hats or pieces of shrimp into diners' open mouths. Every utensil wielded was choreographed to make cool sounds and cut effortlessly through the meat. The chefs often told dumb jokes like, "Do you know how to say you're welcome in Japanese? Don't touch my mustache!" (It's *do itashimashite*, ha ha.) The food was served with either a soy mustard or sesame dipping sauce, and topped off with ice cream and tea. It was good and unbelievably consistent, even today, when there are very few Japanese chefs left at Benihana—they're mostly Latino or white. About a decade ago, when my wife and I went to Benihana for old times' sake, we met a Japanese woman—shock of shocks—who was one of just a couple of women chefs in the entire chain. I sometimes wonder where she went.

*

Growing up, my family used to eat at Benihana for special events—birthdays and holidays, or when out-of-town visitors came to see us in Virginia. Now there are knockoffs of the Benihana concept everywhere, and the experience doesn't seem as novel and fun. Still, Benihana's dipping sauces and salad dressing are very good: My wife, Erin, found convincing recipes in a magazine for both the shoyu and sesame, so we can have them at home anytime.

It's hard to explain now how amazing it was to dine at a restaurant in the 1960s that presented Japanese food as something that regular, everyday Americans could enjoy, and with their entire families no less. Benihana made it "safe" for middle America to like Japanese food, even if it wasn't exactly the dishes that a Japanese in Japan might choose to eat. Rocky Aoki opened the door for Americans to walk through and check out what other dishes Japanese cuisine had to offer. And that's why it's important to include Benihana in a history of Japanese food in America.

Haute cuisine and modern trends

Going back to the two-way exchange of food cultures, it's worth mentioning that Japanese cuisine has influenced Western dining in a very important way. Not only did the wave of "health food" consciousness lead to Americans learning about tofu and soy beans and Japanese food in general, but the traditional preparation and presentation of Japanese food—regional and seasonal ingredients, displayed carefully as art pieces—was an essential influence on French cooking starting in the seventies and on the wave of "fine dining" that has become the standard for top chefs in the US and around the world ever since.

In a research paper published in *Gastronomica* in 2020 Pomona

College professor Sam Yamashita wrote about what he calls the "Japanese turn" in dining and its connection to the *nouvelle cuisine* movement in French cooking. The Japanese government began sending chefs from Japanese culinary schools to France in the early 1970s to study with the top chefs there. When they returned, they were imbued with the modern idea of French cuisine, not unlike the chefs of the Meiji period. "Nouvelle cuisine affirmed much of what Japanese chefs had been taught to value, such as the importance of using and respecting the very freshest ingredients in season and being open to experimentation," Yamashita wrote.

The French chefs themselves were profoundly affected and inspired by the way Japanese chefs approached their craft. Diners could see the cross-pollination in the small servings of carefully prepared and beautifully presented dishes that became common in fine dining in the eighties and nineties and continuing to the present day. That influence was seen in the best restaurateurs in Los Angeles, San Francisco, and New York as well as in Paris, according to professor Yamashita.

This relationship to modern restaurant cuisines can also be seen in *izakaya*-style eateries in the US. An izakaya is basically a place where one can be and drink sake for a while. Put simply, a bar. Izakaya have existed for centuries in Japan. In the old days travelers would stand and drink sake, and eventually the sake barrels were used to sit on and snacks were served. Today, izakaya are popular hangouts for salarymen and women after a long day at the office, where they drink and order small plates of food. As a cultural comparison, think of the 1980s boom in America of tapas bars, where yuppies (young urban professionals, the social equivalent of today's hipsters) would congregate to drink and order small plates of Spanish food.

Japanese food (and culture in general) has had an on-again, off-again love affair with American consumers. While all things Japanese might be chic in one decade, the wartime years made anything Japanese anathema. Along with the explosion of Japanese technology and automobiles in the go-go economy of the sixties and seventies came the racist resentment of Japan's predominance in the eighties. Whenever Japan's relations with the United States are strained, the old stereotypes and hate speech from over a hundred years ago get trotted out as if the "Yellow Peril" of the early twentieth century never went away.

When Japanese immigrants and their American-born children, who were US citizens by birth, were incarcerated during World War II, their culinary traditions were profoundly affected by those years of imprisonment.

JA Ingenuity
A History of Adversity and Adaptation

The food that Japanese Americans grew up on—the common dishes cooked at home and at the Japanese restaurants that mostly served JA communities—aren't always traditional, or washoku, Japanese cuisine. Japanese Americans have adapted their cooking to suit ingredients that are easier to find outside Japan, and as recipes are handed down through generations they evolve to suit the changing tastes of modern living. Japanese Americans have also adjusted recipes to suit non-Japanese palates.

Japanese find that many dishes served in American Japanese restaurants taste too sweet, starting with meat and fish marinated in teriyaki sauce. We usually add more sugar than is typical in Japan. And that's true of other cuisines in America—Korean marinades, potato salad, and even Thai dishes are served sweeter than across the Pacific. I asked a Thai restaurant owner if he and his family changed their recipes to make the dishes sweeter, and he said absolutely: "Americans won't eat it if it's not sweet. Too sweet for us."

This process of sweetening for American customers in a restaurant is one thing, but for Japanese Americans the recipes remained close to the original when cooking at home.

With the passing of generations, however, there may have been less emphasis on cooking Japanese food for family meals. One major reason is that women, who did most of the cooking at home, began to work in the postwar boom years of the sixties and beyond. Maybe June Cleaver could be a full-time housewife in the *Leave It To Beaver*, *Father Knows Best* fifties, and even through the sixties and seventies, television families featured stay-at-home moms. It wasn't until the eighties, when Meredith Baxter Birney played a mom who was an architect in *Family Ties*, and Phylicia Rashad played lawyer Claire Huxtable in *The Cosby Show*, that television caught up. But in real life, mothers in the fifties and sixties were joining the workforce.

Japanese American families with their strong family ties weren't immune from the changing times, and having moms working meant that grandmas may have been the primary cook for some families' meals. Modern foods created for convenience became as standard as they did for many American families: TV dinners, frozen chicken pot pies, chicken a la king in a pouch that you "cooked" by dropping it into boiling water.

When my family moved to the US, it was before American fast food chains invaded Japan. So I got my first taste of McDonald's, Jack in the Box, and Shakey's Pizza when we settled in northern Virginia. And although my mom kept cooking her mix of Japanese and American food at home (and my dad grilled steaks on a small hibachi grill on the back porch—not the typical, bulbous American barbecue grill), we also had frozen dinners and treated fast food as a special night out.

We'd all clamber into our 1967 Plymouth Fury and dad would drive us to Leesburg, twenty minutes down Route 7 from Sterling Park, the *Wonder Years*-style suburban development that had sprung up near the newly built Dulles Airport, where we lived in a one-story ranch house. We'd have a lavish meal sitting in our car in the parking lot of a sparkling-new and exciting ... McDonald's.

And we were new arrivals to America—which is to say, Japanese Americans throughout the country had had many decades to absorb and assimilate the foods and fads that made up the American culinary landscape. If you lived in LA, you may have been eating at McDonalds, maybe even the original location in Downey, California, since the 1950s.

That never meant that JAs no longer ate Japanese food. It meant that like all immigrants to the US, we found ways of juggling our traditional culture, including what we eat, with the new world of pop culture and food that was available to us. And, like with every other thread running through the Japanese American tapestry, we adapted. Dishes—if you can call them that—such as Weenie Royale (cut-up hot dogs mixed with scrambled eggs and soy sauce, served over rice) and the Hawaii-born Spam musubi are emblematic of the malleability of Japanese American cuisine.

Japanese Americans' wartime experience

There's no greater example of this adaptability than during the period of Japanese American incarceration during World War II, when 110,000 people of Japanese ancestry (more than half born in the US and therefore American citizens) were detained in camps. Camp life during World War II changed the diets of Japanese Americans, even as they tried to hold onto some traditions like Oshogatsu and retain some staples of the Japanese diet.

Tofu, miso, and soy sauce were made in some camps toward the end of the war, with prisoners growing soy beans themselves. At Manzanar, some intrepid imprisoned Japanese Americans made tofu and miso from the soy beans and even brewed hydrolyzed vegetable protein (HVP) soy sauce, the type that La Choy and—after the war—Chun King manufactured, because it didn't require the time-consuming fermentation. The camp soy sauce only took a few days to produce.

This was typical JA adaptability.

Not only did Japanese Americans use their agricultural know-how to grow staples like soy and rice, they took what was available from American pantries (or what was supplied by the US Army Quartermaster Corps, which was in charge of bringing in food for the camps) and adapted it in ways that made it more palatable to Japanese tastes. Fried baloney tasted better with soy sauce drizzled on it. Ketchup could be a base for soups. In fact, ketchup became an indispensable condiment and ingredient for dishes, not just a topping for burgers and hot dogs. To this day, we pour ketchup with shoyu on stuffed peppers. Ketchup on rice is an essential ingredient for Japanese chicken rice and *omuraisu*, fried rice mixed with ketchup, topped with a thin omelet.

The influence of the US military was also felt in other foods that were once familiar, if not so popular anymore, to typical Americans: Spam, canned corned beef hash, Vienna sausages—all undoubtedly are seared in the memories of generations of American kids raised in military families. But JA families prepared these items with a twist. Spam made such an impact that Spam musubi was invented, an island cuisine evolution.

Other concentration camp food didn't sit so well with some Japanese Americans. Some older JAs after the war recoiled at the thought of cottage cheese because they were fed the curds so often. The Japanese diet traditionally didn't have a lot of milk or cheese anyway, because many Asians are lactose intolerant.

Some accounts by incarcerees recall being fed mutton—sheep meat—a lot and claim it was often spoiled. Now they can't stand the thought of mutton. And depending on the location, some prisoners were given too much of a good thing. When JAs first arrived at Jerome, the concentration camp near Bayou Bartholomew in Arkansas, they got a treat: tempura freshwater shrimp (or crawfish), which were cheap and plentiful in the swampy waterways near the camp. But having it day after day turned them off to crustaceans.

JAs in concentration camps were allowed to celebrate one traditional Japanese holiday, Oshogatsu, or New Year's Day, every year. They scraped together whatever ingredients they could to approximate the dishes they'd grown up with in the prewar years, and even pounded sticky rice—a traditional communal task—to make mochi for the occasion.

Hawaii

When Hawaii became a state in 1959, it was already one of the most bicultural places in America for US-Japan relations. Before World

War II, it had been a destination for immigrants from Japan for more than fifty years. It was the closest stop for Japanese laborers in the late 1800s in search of a better life, and the first stop for emigrants heading on to the United States. By 1920, almost half of the population of Hawaii was Japanese. When Pearl Harbor was bombed on December 7, 1941, and the Pacific War began, there were so many people of Japanese heritage—both immigrants and Hawaiian-born (who would count as US citizens by birth since Hawaii was a territory of the United States)—that, unlike Japanese and Japanese Americans on the West Coast of the mainland, they couldn't all be locked away in concentration camps. The economy would have shut down. So although entire families lost their homes, farms, and businesses and were incarcerated on the mainland, most Japanese and Japanese Americans on Hawaii were treated the same as other residents, observing wartime curfews

"Family Owned and Operated"

. . . .

My family owned and operated one of the very first Japanese restaurants in Minneapolis. (Tokyo Restaurant in Dinkytown, Minneapolis.) The restaurant was opened by my father's immigrant uncle, Norio Kirihara, in 1960. At the time it opened, there was only one other Japanese restaurant in this area. I worked there as a dishwasher and cook in my high school and college years as did my older brother. My mom worked there as a waitress and my father did the books. My father's aunt and his mother also worked there many years. It was located right next to the University of Minnesota campus and it was frequented by university students and staff from all over the world. It closed after my father's uncle died in the early eighties.

Randy Kirihara

JAPANESE AMERICAN WARTIME IMPRIS-ONMENT: (*top left*) A group of Japanese American children enjoy ice cream during their imprisonment at the Santa Anita detention facility. (*bottom left*) A family together at Manzanar. Despite their imprisonment, JAs adapted many traditions and foods to camp life. (*above*) A general store in Maui, Hawaii, in operation since 1929. Far fewer were imprisoned in Hawaii than on the mainland. Most of the population of Hawaii at the time was of Japanese origin. (*right*) A Japanese American farm worker and his daughter enjoying a cream soda. This picture was taken in 1942, the same year incarceration began.

and rationing. Those who were imprisoned were sent to one long-term prison, Honouliuli on Oahu, which held people of Japanese heritage from 1943 to 1946. The camp was forgotten and covered over by vegetation until it was rediscovered half a century later and named a historic landmark site.

There's a wonderful mix in Hawaii of traditional Japanese food culture with Polynesian and native Hawaiian, plus Chinese, Filipino, and Korean cuisines, with a layer of American military on top. The most familiar fusion food that is a combination of Japanese and American is Spam musubi, which uses a slice of the canned meat Spam, a standard military-issue food, on a block of rice, wrapped with *nori* seaweed. The Spam is usually pan-fried with a little soy sauce or teriyaki sauce and might or might not have seasoning like *furikake*, a condiment sprinkled over rice, mixed in, or Tabasco or sriracha sauce drizzled on for a little kick.

Spam caught on big in Hawaii in part because of the influence of the US military, and Spam has also spread to other places with a large military presence, including Korea and Okinawa in Japan. In Okinawa, the American influence has led to a local specialty, *tako-raisu* (taco rice), taco meat with lettuce and tomatoes served over rice instead of on a corn tortilla shell. The dish was invented by local cooks to attract the GIs stationed on Okinawa. There's that two-way cross-cultural exchange again.

Hawaiians have bent culinary rules as a matter of course. You can find chili served over spaghetti, or loco moco, a hamburger patty served on a mound of rice and topped with a fried egg, with a lava of brown gravy poured over the entire thing. Another Hawaiian spin on Japanese food is saimin, the state's unique and ubiquitous take on ramen or soba (more on that later). Sekiya's Restaurant and Delicatessen in Honolulu has been cooking up saimin and other

Japanese/Hawaiian comfort foods as well as diner faves, like burgers and fountain drinks, since 1935.

Japanese Americans in the culinary world

This continual willingness to adapt to local seasonal ingredients—or lack of them—is evident with the current crop of notable chefs of Japanese heritage. As the *New York Times* noted in a 2019 article about the Japanese chefs who are modernizing the cuisine while still honoring their heritage, the younger generation of top restaurateurs are expanding the boundaries of what's considered "Japanese cuisine." For example, Brooklyn chef Patch Troffer's cooking isn't so much an innovation as it is an homage to his Japanese grandmother, who married an American GI during the Korean War and lived in South Carolina, where Japanese ingredients were as rare as konbu in Pueblo, Colorado. She made dashi soup stock with canned clams. And made it work, obviously, because she inspired her grandson, who substitutes horseradish root for wasabi in his restaurant.

Italian cuisine also gets the Japanized treatment from young and adventurous chefs, with US-born, Japan-raised Los Angeles chef Keiichiro Kurobe's Blackship (a reference to the "Black Ships" that Matthew Perry sailed into Tokyo Bay in the 1850s to demand Japan open up to the world), which serves Italian pasta with Japanese flourishes. Think carbonara ramen. . . .

Another young JA chef who was born and raised in LA, Niki Nakayama, has made a splash and become nationally known for her n/naka restaurant in Los Angeles. She serves thirteen-course kaiseki meals that sound traditional in name, with courses like *shiizakana* (fish) and *niku* (meat), but the seafood dish might feature spaghetti noodles with abalone, truffles, and cod roe. Nakayama worked at a top Japanese restaurant before taking several years off to travel, eat, and learn in Japan. She immersed herself in the traditional art of kaiseki cuisine while working with a master chef at a *ryokan*, a traditional Japanese inn, in a small hot springs village northwest of Tokyo. Now she's bringing that artful knowledge to the bustle and varied fare in the heart of urban Southern California.

These JA chefs are mixing it up in ways their ancestors would have never, ever expected—miso in Texas barbecue? Cocoa powder in curry? What?

This willingness to adapt to their situations, not just sociopolitical but geographic, has been a hallmark of the evolution of JA foods. And one product perfectly reflects this edible ethic: Karami Salsa.

Karami is a Japanese American twist on salsa that tastes pretty great on a lot of food, including chips, meats, and fish, but its origins are as a Japanese side dish, *tsukudani*, the kind you might see served next to or atop rice.

Karami, which means "beautiful heat," has a salty, savory vegetable base that's enhanced with a subtly sweet flavor and a mildly spicy kick. You can't put a finger on one overarching taste, which makes it a perfect example of the Japanese word umami, which translates as "pleasant savory taste" and is considered one of the five basic tastes following sweet, sour, bitter, and salty. It's a Japanese concept that's perfectly embodied in a spoonful of Karami.

What makes it Japanese American, not Japanese?

According to Karami's history, the salsa was first made as a side dish in the 1890s, when Japanese arrived in Colorado from the West Coast to pursue jobs on railroads and settle on farms. As the men who came first brought their wives and started families, they adapted recipes to available ingredients in the landlocked state.

So in southern Colorado when they began making vegetable side dishes, instead of using konbu or *wakame* seaweed, which was a wistful memory of life along the Pacific Ocean, they experimented with various ingredients . . . until they tried Pueblo's famous green chile. The roasted chile added the texture of wakame, but when mixed with soy sauce and sugar it gave a nice kick and the hard-to-describe umami to vegetables.

So Japanese Americans raised in Colorado since then have had the familiar flavor of this treat served on their tables. If a JA family is from California (and arrived in Colorado after the WWII incarceration camps) or lives along the West Coast now, Karami may be a novel flavor. The family of the company's late founder Justin Takaki has lived in Pueblo for generations (his father was mayor of Pueblo in the 1970s), and he's the one who introduced a business partner to his family's recipe for Karami.

I found the taste very familiar, though as a side dish, not a salsa. Erin's family loved it when I had them try it, even though they had never quite had the mix of sweet and spicy served this way.

But a woman from one Japanese American family that's lived in northern Colorado's farm country for generations knew immediately what I was describing. She said her grandmother could probably cook up some green chiles into something like Karami today, because she made a dish with green chiles, sugar, soy sauce, and vegetables.

I love the flavor of Karami, but I also love the story behind it. It's a true Japanese American invention, from before the wartime incarceration, adapted out of necessity with traditional recipes. I hope the family continues to make and sell this unique salsa.

*

Green chiles are admittedly a surprising ingredient for Japanese food. But one plant that JAs eat that would make Japanese diners jealous is the matsutake, the aromatic mushroom that grows in the loose soil under the shade of the *matsu*, or pine tree. Japanese Americans have always hunted for matsutake in the late summer and early fall—they're especially plentiful in the Rocky Mountains of Colorado and Wyoming, while in Japan it's become rare and expensive.

Matsutake hunting could be both a solo explorer adventure (one Japanese chef I know goes to his spot every year alone and brings back bags of the flavorful shrooms) or a fun family outing. You might guess from the chef's solo hunting trips that the locations for the most plentiful matsutake are kept to oneself—the old saying "If I told you, I'd have to kill you" is not just a cliche, it's practically a rule.

My wife remembers heading up to favorite family locales each year and filling up big *kome* (rice) bags with mushrooms she'd pick. The outing was like a picnic—musubi or rice balls were prepared along with American snacks. Although sometimes things can get out of hand—my mom got separated from her group of friends one year and got lost; the sheriff's department was called to search the mountainside until my mom was found!

JAs have been taught to leave the ground as they found it—if they dig up a matsutake, they pat the extra soil off and place it back in the hole, and carefully replace the pine needles and leaves to cover the spot so more mushrooms can grow back. In recent years, the harvest has become smaller because of competition from people who aren't hunting matsutake for themselves and their family and friends, but so they can sell it to markets for ridiculously high profits. Those profits are even crazier in Japan, where the cost of matsutake can reach truffle territory: $1,000 to $2,000 per pound. In American markets you can usually find matsutake for $40, but they really taste so much better if you plucked them for free off the mountainside.

Instead of hunting them for profit, JAs brought the matsutake home, washed them, and cut them before putting them in bags and freezing them for use throughout the year as an earthy, flavorful addition to miso soup or sliced or chopped and cooked with rice for *matsutake gohan*.

History through cookbooks

One revealing way to track the changing taste of Japanese Americans over the years has been to read—and use—the many cookbooks that Japanese American communities have published over the decades. Before the war and incarceration, it seems that family recipes were stored only in the heads of the mothers and chefs of Japanese American homes and restaurants. I have a collection of cookbooks beginning in the 1960s, although earlier cookbooks probably were published, that reflect evolving cuisines collected by (mostly, though not exclusively) women involved with churches, temples, and community organizations.

The *Nisei Favorites* cookbook of the Gardena Valley Baptist Church's Women's Missionary Society has been reprinted numerous times. The 1966 version I have has yellowed pages and ads for a Japanese American realtor, a JA-owned pharmacy, and JA salesmen at a Chevy auto dealership, as well as an ad for

"Strong Feminist That She Was"

. . . .

My mom was a nurse in the army during the Korean War. Because of this, she was allowed entrance to the American Legion Post No. 185 (in Denver), also known as the Nisei Post. She was even the Commander of the post at one point. For the annual potluck it was customary to ask the wives of the post members to bring food. Someone called the house to let my mom know that she was assigned *onigiri*. Being the strong feminist that she was, she said, "Great! I'll let Ben (my dad) know." And while my dad wasn't happy about this, he made and brought onigiri with *umeboshi*.

Jane Miyahara

"Vintage-Flavor" Kikkoman soy sauce that displayed the *Good Housekeeping* seal of approval. The most recently published cookbook I have is the Seattle JACL chapter's *Bento Box Cookbook* of 2007. The eighth printing of the St. Louis JACL chapter's *Nisei Kitchen* collection of recipes, originally published in 1975, was in 2008. *Generation to Generation: A Family Cookbook* was first published by the Orange County Buddhist Church in Anaheim, California in 1984; the copy I have was printed in 1996. In most of these cookbooks, the person who submitted the recipe is credited, a sign that many people who purchased or were given these books probably knew at least some of the cooks who shared their dishes.

The *Takahashi Family Cookbook* was printed for a 1989 family reunion by family friends of my in-laws. The Denver Buddhist Temple's Buddhist Women's association published the *Treasured Recipes* cookbook in 1978. The Brighton Nisei Women's Club's *Eastern Western Food* was originally published in 1960, and its fourth edition was printed in 2004. *A Taste of Heaven—Favorites Yesterday*

& Today was assembled in 1995 for the sixty-fifth anniversary of the West Los Angeles United Methodist Church.

These cookbooks are both markers for the organizations that gathered the recipes as well as food-memory time machines for anyone who turns to the recipes and brings them to life.

Peoples' tastes have changed over the years, and you can see how cooking has evolved with the passage of time. The oldest books often list "Ajinomoto," the brand of MSG that many JAs grew up with, as an ingredient. Some later books skip the brand name and just list "MSG." many recent recipes don't include any MSG, probably reflecting the controversy over the umami-inducing ingredient and its modern unpopularity. The Brighton Nisei Women's Club reflects the changing times by listing in its glossary "Aji-no-moto," "Accent" (the American brand sold by B&G Foods, the company that also owns Ortega Mexican products, Cream of Wheat, Crisco, Green Giant, Weber Grills, and Einstein Bagels, just to name a few), and the scientific name Monosodium Glutamate, and explains the products are "flavor enhancers."

A review of JA cookbooks also proves the wide-ranging culinary curiosity of Japanese families over the decades after coming to America. Because *issei* immigrants were often employed as domestic workers if they were women, they learned to cook for white families and also learned recipes from other domestic workers including African American and Latinx women. Therefore, the cookbooks all consistently include not just the nostalgic traditional foods of Japan, but all sorts of dishes that suggest multicultural family gastronomies.

Flipping through pages you could find listings for "Smokie Links with Candy Apple Sauce" followed by "Kikkoman Shoyu Wieners," "Fried Chicken," and "Skillet Barbecue Chicken." Or you could find "Tacos Supreme," "Oven Lau Lau (Hawaiian Pork Roast with Butterfish and Spinach)," and "Italian Quiche." In one book, "Pasta Primavera" and "Potato Kani Koroke" (potato crab croquette) are on the same page. In another, "Tamale Pie" shares space with "Beef and Bean Sprouts" and "Beef Lo Mein." One of our favorite cookbooks, which has sticky notes and markers poking out of many of its pages, posits "Jing-Du Spareribs," "Sweet and Sour Pork," "Barbecue Baby Rib Pork" (with soy sauce in addition to a brand of barbecue sauce), "Kombu Maki with Pork," and "Chili Verde" and "Pork Green Chili" together in one cross-cultural, pan-Pacific stream.

Some cookbooks had entire sections for Chinese food—that's how intertwined the early success of Chinese cuisine in America had become with Japanese families' dining options. In fact, for many Japanese American communities, Chinese restaurants were the go-to locales for large family and community events such as banquets or weddings and after funerals. Chinese restaurants were equipped to better serve large crowds, and the food was simpler to serve on a Lazy Susan. The rotating tray that makes it easy to share food around a table was an American invention but became *de rigueur* for Chinese eateries, which accommodated large groups of diners. I can't count the number of annual banquets I've enjoyed at Chinese restaurants for JA and Asian American organizations, especially scheduled during the Lunar New Year season. Sometimes I've had several of the same multi-course meals at the same popular Chinese restaurant on multiple weekends. Good thing I like Chinese almost as much as I like Japanese food!

Many of the books also include handfuls of Hawaiian dishes ("Haupia Coconut Pudding" in *Nisei Kitchen*, for example), and Korean standards such as "Kim Chee" and "Korean Beef" are common entries.

But at their core, these cookbooks preserved and passed on the traditional foods of the issei generation, albeit perhaps with some necessary American substitutions for ingredients. Some include unusual dishes that harken back to early immigrant community recipes. The St. Louis JACL's *Nisei Kitchen* cookbook explains how to make flat cakes of translucent konnyaku from mountain yam powder . . . using lye, with helpful hints like what types of containers to avoid, how to clean up the lye, and "If you are working alone, place the container on the floor against a cabinet door for support when adding the lye to the thickened konnyaku." I just buy premade konnyaku at the Japanese supermarket, thank you!

One cookbook has helpful illustrations and text for younger generations of JAs on how to use chopsticks and other basic Japanese cooking tips.

Sukiyaki, teriyaki, and tempura of course all make appearances. (However, tempura wasn't included in the most recent of the books, the 2007 *Bento Box Cookbook* from Seattle.)

Chashu, the Japanese version of Chinese *char siu* roasted pork, is a popular item that seems to appear in most collections of JA recipes.

All the cookbooks are bound to have some Chinese American or Chinese-influenced recipes, but you can tell the more modern compilations—they include recipes beyond old-school American Chinese food and include more diverse dishes like "Nuoc Nam," a Vietnamese fish sauce condiment, or fusion-mashup concoctions like "Chinese Five Spice Oatmeal Cookies."

The classic Weenie Royale shows up in an older cookbook sans egg as "Kikkoman Shoyu Wieners," basically hot dogs glazed with shoyu, sugar, sake, and Ajinomoto. Sounds pretty delicious, actually.

So Japanese Americans who grew up in postwar America were fed traditional Japanese food, but also the expanded palettes of Chinese, Korean, Hawaiian, and of course American recipes. And increasingly, JAs ate as typical Americans did in the fifties, sixties, and beyond: As the convenience of frozen foods arrived to help harried, on-the-go families prepare meals, we were happy to sit in front of our television sets and gobble up chicken pot pies and TV dinners. That was also the era when fast food chains appeared and changed the way all Americans ate, again, on the go. McDonald's was a revelation when we first had it in the mid-sixties after moving to the States. Pizza was a godsend, food designed for social interaction with friends (well, at least the full pizza pies—the New York–style single slices were still a solitary dining experience).

But Japanese food still carried cultural weight. For many JA families, for special celebrations, including birthdays or entertaining out-of-town visitors, a favorite local Japanese restaurant was a unanimous choice. For many of us, Benihana, even though it wasn't exactly "authentic" or "traditional," was a popular destination because it was tasty, made for good interaction at the large, shared teppanyaki tables, and was just plain fun. So who cared if the chefs were increasingly not Japanese (or even trained in Japan), or told the same corny jokes as they flipped shrimp into your mouth?

This was what Japanese American food was like in the days before sushi became a common American food.

5 Rolling On

If You Knew Sushi Like I Knew Sushi . . .

Sushi is the most iconic dish on the menu of Japanese cuisine today—it's what most people think of when they think Japanese food—but it took a long time for it to reach the level of familiarity that it enjoys in America now. Its popularity is still skyrocketing: One survey found almost 4,000 restaurants in the US served sushi in 2017, but one business tracking study found that number had exploded to almost 18,000 in 2021.

Like many Asian American kids who ate with white friends in school cafeterias, I heard tiresome comments like, "Eeeew, you eat raw fish? That's gross!" Yeah, but I bet you guys and your kids all love sushi now, even the not-so-authentic sushi sold in supermarket chains. Progress comes slowly, but eventually does arrive if you're patient.

Sushi may have been around in Japan for centuries and in the

United States for decades, but in the 1980s, it was not a familiar food to most Americans.

A perfect example of sushi's status was shown in director John Hughes's 1985 "Brat Pack" film *The Breakfast Club*, starring a group of then-young Hollywood actors on the precipice of becoming celebrities (okay, most of them didn't have very long or distinguished careers). Molly Ringwald, who was only seventeen in real life at the time, played a snooty, privileged high school student stuck in detention with kids from other school cliques, including a juvenile delinquent played by Judd Nelson. During lunch, Ringwald brings a wooden tray out from a paper bag, followed by a lacquer box, and, improbably, a bottle of soy sauce with the pour spout uncovered.

Nelson watches her after making a lewd remark, then asks, "What's that?"

"Sushi," Ringwald replies.

"Sushi?" the punk asks.

"Rice, raw fish, and seaweed."

"You won't accept a guy's tongue in your mouth but you'll eat that?"

This was how sushi was introduced to many Americans.

Americans' relationship to Japan and Japanese culture has often been affected by the cyclical whims of popular culture. In the 1999 video for her hit song "Nothing Really Matters," the singer Madonna wore a red kimono and said in interviews that she had been inspired by the bestselling novel *Memoirs of a Geisha*. She reflected the Japan fad of the day, which led to a season of Japan-themed shopping at one of New York's posh, high-fashion department stores. Twenty years earlier in September 1980, the TV miniseries *Shogun*, based on the 1975 James Clavell novel of the same name, was a huge hit and dominated the airwaves (and subsequent award shows). And some culture critics think it opened the door for Americans to try sushi and other, more adventurous Japanese foods.

I had read the book while in college (in New York City, no less) and felt the Japan fad of the time. The Japanese Artists Association in New York even saw the opportunity and held a gallery show in SoHo, the hipster district of Manhattan. I happened to be a painting student at Pratt Institute at the time and had been invited to join this group of mostly artists from Japan—even though I was about as white as all my punk-rock-loving friends in art school. Amazingly, I sold a painting from that gallery show ... to American playwright Edward Albee. When I got a call from him in my dorm apartment on a Sunday morning asking if I was the one who'd painted the piece in the SoHo gallery show, I thought it was a prank by friends and almost hung up on him when he said he was Edward Albee. "Oh yeah, sure, like the playwright?"

"Um, yes."

But, I digress. I devoured *Shogun* during my spare time at art school and later eagerly tuned in to watch the 1980 five-part mini-series.

As a Japanese American who was born in Tokyo and raised in the US, I identified with both sides of the narrative about an Englishman who is captured on a Dutch ship in feudal Japan and eventually becomes a samurai to a fictional version of the real-life shogun who would unify Japan. The TV mini-series even more than James Clavell's novel sparked a serious Japanophile frenzy across the United States. It was filmed entirely in Japan and all the Japanese characters were played by actual Japanese actors, not white actors in yellowface. The main protagonist, the naval navigator John Blackthorne, was played by Richard Chamberlain. It had star power and told a compelling dramatic historical story based on real people (even Blackthorne was based on an Englishman who found himself made into a samurai in feudal Japan).

In the wake of *Shogun*, Americans were fascinated by Japan, both the Japan of the past and the present. The book and series became staples of high school and college world history courses. And with that new education and cultural faddism came a curiosity for Japanese cuisine that was more sophisticated than the three foundational dishes—sukiyaki, teriyaki, and tempura—that the West knew in the postwar years, and Japanese restaurants became more common across the country. The feudal era portrayed in *Shogun* was exactly when the Portuguese introduced tempura to Japan, but the show also opened the door for adventurous Americans to try a first taste of sushi.

The origins of sushi

Ironically, sushi wasn't really eaten in its current form during the feudal era of Japan. However, most Americans even today probably wouldn't want to try the original version of sushi, which is still made in rural Japan.

Sushi's origins are in a dish called *funazushi*, which is made of carp that's heavily salted and stored for a year, then mixed with rice and fermented for two or more years. Some people who've tried it say it smells and tastes like strong cheese. You can still try it if you're ever in Japan—it's available throughout the country. The authentic version is made with the *nigorobuna* carp in Lake Biwa, northeast of Kyoto. Travel to Lake Biwa and you can try it with the locals who've eaten it for centuries. This process of fermenting fish with salt and rice was originally brought to Japan from China—it was a way of preserving fish, and it's still done in parts of Japan, where *saba*, or mackerel, is fermented with salt and rice bran.

Over centuries, Japanese adapted this idea and, instead of using it as a way of preserving fish to be consumed later, began eating slightly fermented fish with rice as a dish. The arrival of rice vinegar made it possible to eliminate the excessive salt that had been used to ferment fish and made today's sushi possible. By the Edo period, the period of rule by the Tokugawa shogunate, when Tokyo was called Edo, sushi began to take on a more modern form. It was considered fast food—not fancy Japanese cuisine.

Edomae sushi (Edo sushi) was assembled by food-cart street vendors who took marinated or lightly cooked fish and mixed it into rice with vegetables and other ingredients so the fish and rice could be eaten together. It was called *hayazushi*, or "fast sushi"— Japanese fast food! Nigiri sushi, as we know it today, with fish placed on top of a hand-molded piece of rice, evolved in the early 1800s in Tokyo, though raw fish wasn't the standard until refrigeration technology came along to make it safe to eat sashimi. Also during the Edo period, *inarizushi* (sushi rice placed in a pouch of

"I Want Sushi!"

My daughter Simone started eating sushi pretty much as soon as she was able to eat solid food— because her mom and I loved it. In fact, for her second birthday, I asked her, "Simone, do you want Noodles & Company for your birthday dinner? And she gave me a look of contempt she perfected in her teen years and replied, "No, daddy! I want sushi!"

Eric Elkins

fried tofu skin) and various forms of *maki* and *chirashizushi* (a variety of sashimi scattered over a bowl of sushi rice) caught on. All are still served in sushi shops today. My mom's favorite Japanese dish of all time is chirashizushi.

One other reason that Japanese restaurants serving sushi began to blossom after the popularity of *Shogun* was that Japan's economy was exploding and companies were expanding globally, with Japanese employees being sent worldwide to support their booming businesses.

That meant that Japanese workers—salarymen as well as their bosses—sent to work in the US were homesick for authentic Japanese eats, including sushi. Some restaurants in America added sushi bars but they initially mostly attracted Japanese diners. Raw fish was still a bit too exotic for mainstream Americans.

The rise of sushi in America

It would be a couple more decades before sushi really caught on with the public, but by the mid-eighties, as shown in *The Breakfast Club*, sushi was a symbol of the culinary elite, a food eaten by celebrities and yuppies. A 1988 *Esquire* cover story with the headline "The Days of Wine and Sushi" shows actor Michael J. Fox, "Yupper Classman," dining on a plate of nigiri sushi. He was hot and hip. And he gave sushi a national thumbs-up.

But even as late as the 1990s, when I was the entertainment editor at a daily newspaper, I learned that my predecessor, who happened to also be Japanese American, preferred burgers to sushi because he thought sushi in general, and raw fish in particular, was gross.

The jokey pop culture references like Judd Nelson's in *The*

Breakfast Club continued for at least another decade, though it would be hard to get away with a sushi joke today. Even back then, sushi was making its inexorable invasion of the Western palate.

The hit TV show *Friends* aired an episode in 2000 in which the character Ross, played by David Schwimmer, lies to his pals Rachel and Phoebe, who are taking a martial arts class, and says he's taken years of karate and that he has developed "Unagi," which he says is a sense of one's surroundings, "a state of total awareness." The women reply "isn't that a kind of sushi?", which shows that sushi has made an impact on some hipsters' awareness, but not everyone's. The episode continues with Ross trying to scare the women just to prove his mistaken point.

A *Saturday Night Live* skit in 2003 made fun of "Al Sharpton's Casa de Sushi." And to prove its cultural acceptance, *Saturday Night Live* revisited sushi in 2006 with a skit starring guest host Matt Dillon, "How to Order Sushi Like a CEO," in which a bumbling businessman tries to impress viewers with a pitch for his new book by stumbling his way through types of sushi and sashimi. The humor in the script depends on the audience's familiarity with sushi themselves.

In 1999, a series of television commercials that became a pop culture phenomenon even included a sushi theme in one popular spot. Budweiser's "Whassup?" campaign, which featured friends asking each other "what's up?" became so popular that the beer company came up with variations for several years. One of the most memorable showed the star of the campaign, a character named Dookie, out dining at a sushi restaurant. The server brings his plate and says, "Here you are, sushi . . . and [on a separate plate] wasabi."

Dookie grins and mutters "wasabi." The server responds, "Yeah, wasabi," upon which Dookie takes off on a variation of "wasabi" just like he's done with his friends for "whassup"—all the sushi bar chefs yell out "Waasabi!" in unison and everyone starts saying the word, until his girlfriend slams her hand on the table and the commercial ends. The joke wouldn't work unless viewers knew what wasabi was and that it's served with sushi.

But the ultimate sign of the acceptance of sushi has been its availability in supermarket chains across the US—often in designated sushi counters offering up freshly assembled and rolled sushi, albeit not too adventurous styles.

The path to the appearance of supermarket sushi counters, from Texas to Alaska and New York to Los Angeles, followed in the footsteps of sushi bars at Japanese restaurants. That journey had its earliest trailblazers in cities that boasted large and active Japanese immigrant communities, including New York and Los Angeles but also West Coast enclaves like San Francisco and Seattle. People who had lived in Japan and moved to the US knew the pleasures of *nigirizushi*, the hand-formed ovals of vinegared rice topped with a slice of raw fish.

But this was the postwar America of *Leave It to Beaver* and Elvis Presley. While The King was feasting on extravagant American food in the late 1970s, some Japanese restaurants across the country were starting to put in sushi bars to begin serving sushi to people who wouldn't know *maguro* from mutton.

A Japanese immigrant named Moto Saito was the pioneer who broke the raw fish barrier, putting sushi on the menu at her Midtown New York restaurant, named Saito, in 1957 and teaching non-Japanese diners how to eat sashimi and sushi. Like many Japanese restaurateurs in the US, then as now, Saito wore kimono as she floated through the restaurant, giving an air of cultural appropriateness and authenticity to calm the jittery nerves of curious but frightened *gaijin*.

Kawafuku in Los Angeles's Little Tokyo district is credited as the first well-known eatery to serve sushi beyond the Japanese immigrant and business clientele by adding a sushi bar (reportedly the first use of the term "sushi bar") in 1966. But the huge signage on the top floor of the building still proclaimed the main dish as "Sukiyaki" to anyone driving by.

More adventurous restaurants jumped on the sushi boat starting in 1970. That year saw more sushi restaurants opening in LA, including one next to a movie studio that became a favorite spot for stars.

Seattle's pioneering eatery Maneki, one of the oldest continuous Japanese restaurants in the United States, opened in 1904. Though it was shut temporarily during World War II, while its owners were interned, it reopened in a new location a few blocks away in Seattle's International District after the war (the original building had been vandalized while the restaurant was closed). Maneki hired a sushi chef from Japan and put a sushi bar in the front of the room in 1972.

New York City's cutting-edge gastro-explorers and celebs got a couple of sushi spots too. Inagiku, located inside the Waldorf Astoria, the first sushi restaurant in Midtown Manhattan, opened in 1974 and served the cognoscenti until it closed in 2009.

But most other mom-and-pop restaurants were still more cautious, especially away from the coasts, and waited years longer to add sushi to their menu. Denver's Akebono added a sushi bar in the 1990s. By then a couple of other area Japanese restaurants were also serving sushi.

One of the the Denver area's early adopters wasn't even a Japanese restaurant. An American seafood restaurant called Pelican Pete's added a small sushi bar along one wall in the 1980s. The Japanese chefs who worked there eventually went off to start various pioneering sushi bars of their own in Colorado. My dad somehow learned about Pelican Pete's and we ate there regularly. Our family took up all the seats at the bar and we'd hang out eating for a couple of hours. I expected the checks would easily top a hundred dollars (back then, that was a lot) but we always seemed to get our dinners at a discount. They must have liked having customers who could speak Japanese and appreciate the subtleties of quality sushi.

✳

Growing up in Japan, sushi was a luxury. My mom made it, but mostly for special occasions like Oshogatsu. We would go out to restaurants for sushi, but again, mostly for special family occasions.

Really, more often than sushi, we would have sashimi, just the sliced raw fish, served with soy sauce and wasabi, with rice and miso soup to complete the meal. And for handheld rice dishes, we were much more likely to have musubi or *onigiri*, rice balls that are often shaped by hand, lightly salted, and filled with a little bit of fish or *umeboshi* (salted pickled plums), then wrapped with nori seaweed. Think of them as sushi without the vinegared sushi rice.

I found that Japanese Americans have also always been familiar with sushi and sashimi, but as when I was a child in Japan, it was mostly served for occasions like New Year's. The one sushi that was common—because it's pretty quick and easy to make and doesn't cost much (no sashimi required)—was inari, vinegared rice stuffed into sacks of fried tofu skins. Like onigiri, it's a type of comfort food. Japanese Americans call them "footballs" because, well, they sort of look like footballs.

The other type of sushi that I ate often is *futomaki*, literally "fat rolls." They're around two and a half inches in diameter and include usually six or seven ingredients rolled up in sushi rice and wrapped in nori, but not with the usual raw fish that people expect in *makizushi*, or sushi rolls. Instead, the fish in the futomaki that my mom made was *sakura denbu*, pink shredded and dried sea-soned codfish (maybe accompanied by crab or, more likely, fake Krab), along with thin strips of sweetened egg omelet, spinach, and simmered strips of shiitake mushrooms and the calabash gourd known as *kanpyo*. It takes a lot of preparation but it's a pretty typ-ical style of sushi that my mom used to make, more often than the sashimi-topped ovals of rice that most Americans immediately picture when they think of sushi.

The California roll: an all-American innovation

By far the most famous sushi in America—more so than even the quintessential nigiri—is the California roll. It's become a ubiqui-tous presence in Japanese restaurants, sushi bars, and, yes, super-market sushi trays.

The first time my mom saw a California roll, she scrunched up her face and, with a distinctive sneer, muttered, "Ehhh? *A-reh wah inchiki sushi desu!*" ("Huh? That's fake sushi!") She saw imme-diately that California rolls, whose most obvious feature is the rice on the outside, weren't authentic. To be fair, in the decades since the roll was introduced, it's made its way back to Japan and become

SUSHI, THE MODERN FACE OF JAPANESE FOOD: (*top left*) My aunt Eiko in Nemuro, Hokkaido, serves the freshest *ikura* (salmon roe) you could possibly imagine. It's become a common sight on sushi. (*bottom left*) Sushi Rama in Denver serves modern conveyor sushi in an appropriately modern-looking setting. (*above*) The time comes at the end of the meal at any *kaiten* sushi restaurant to count up the plates and get the check, seen here at Hanamaru in Nemuro. The tab is often less than you'd imagine given the tower you created!

somewhat common in sushi bars there, mostly in places where foreign tourists dine. Many Japanese, as my mom did, consider the California roll a non-Japanese invention.

Which is true: The California roll, though created by a Japanese chef, was made for foreigners—particularly Americans who didn't know Japanese food culture. This *"inchiki sushi"* was made safe for Americans (meaning white people). The reason? Non-Japanese were (1) grossed out by the thought of eating raw fish, and (2) they were grossed out by the nori seaweed on the outside of a sushi roll.

First, the California roll replaced sashimi with cooked crab or *surimi* imitation crab (a Japanese product made of ground fish paste with red coloring, shaped into a "crab stick") and/or avocado, which approximates the texture of *maguro*, tuna, with a more familiar look and flavor. Second, the California roll hid the nori by flipping the order of ingredients in making this type of futomaki—instead of laying down seaweed as the bottom layer, rice is spread out as a bed on the bamboo rolling mat before being covered by seaweed, then the other ingredients are added before being rolled and sliced.

The inventor of this roll is disputed: Sushi chef Hidekazu Tojo in Vancouver, Canada, claims he invented the "Inside Out Roll" in the late 1970s and has received a Japanese Ministry of Agriculture award as Japanese cuisine's Goodwill Ambassador for it. But a Los Angeles chef, Ichiro Mashita, who worked at the restaurant Tokyo Kaikan in LA's Little Tokyo district, reportedly came up with an early version of the California roll in the 1960s, by first replacing tuna with avocado. He claimed he came up with the substitution during the off-season, when *toro*, fatty tuna, wasn't available. His customers at the time weren't sashimi-averse at all, because they were either Japanese, Japanese Americans, or non-Japanese who had traveled or worked in Japan and were familiar with authentic cuisine. By the 1970s, though, even the California rolls in California had evolved to feature the rice on the outside.

The California roll may be something my mom looked at with derision, but it's an incredibly important part of the evolution of Japanese food in the West. It took until the 1980s, but the California roll caught on with a wide array of Americans who wouldn't have tried traditional sushi at all. It was a gateway drug that allowed the curious and more adventurous diner to explore and expand their palate to include the real thing. Now that Americans are comfortable with nori on the outside of sushi, we have a myriad of giant cone-shaped handrolls (the Japanese call them *temaki*) with weird non-traditional ingredients and outrageous names that no doubt would freak out my mom more than the California roll ever did. That's how far sushi has evolved in its worldwide journey.

Tuna and salmon: a recent addition

We think of salmon and tuna as staples of sushi, both in maki and nigiri, but they're somewhat recent additions to the sushi menu.

Tuna, which is prized and popular for both its lean and fatty cuts, can go for millions of dollars at auction in Tokyo's elite fish market. But even as recently as the 1970s, tuna was considered too fatty for Japanese tastes. It took the development of better refrigeration and, crucially, air transport of fresh tuna before it became the star of the sea and Japanese learned to appreciate the fattier belly cuts *chutoro* and *otoro*. Believe it or not, those fatty parts of tuna were used primarily for cat food back then, and tuna meat in general was destined to be canned. That's why American baby boomers think first of cans of Starkist and Chicken of the Sea when tuna is mentioned. During the peak popularity of New England sport fishing in the mid-twenieth century, 400-pound bluefin tuna were used for trophy photos, then disposed of in trash dumps or tossed back into the ocean to rot and provide fodder for other fish to feed on. As the Japanese would say today, *"mottainai!"* ("How wasteful!"). But tuna's bloody-red flesh was considered too strong-tasting and smelly, especially to be eaten raw.

As tastes evolved and refrigeration and freezing technology made it easier to keep fish fresh, tuna, including the bluefin, became a delicacy in a few short decades. Since the 1990s, when sushi became mainstream in the United States and tuna became the most popular raw fish to consume, the bluefin population in particular has been decimated.

Likewise salmon, a popular fish for centuries in Japan, was always eaten cooked, on a grill or pan-fried, smoked, or cured, never raw. That's because Pacific salmon carried parasites that could make people sick. But cutting-edge diners in the US ate salmon (a *New York Times* article in the mid-1970s noted salmon as nigiri sushi available in restaurants, and a 1981 article mentions how salmon is one of the fish available for sashimi in the city).

In Japan, though, salmon was still considered junk fish in its raw state even as recently as the 1990s. Once again, it took modern refrigeration technology and farming techniques—and a brilliant marketing campaign by Norway, across the globe from Japan—before salmon could join the list of fish on a sushi menu.

Japanese seafood overall faced decreasing production from overfishing and restrictions from the United Nations on where Japanese were allowed to fish. Meanwhile, in the 1970s Norway had a glut of farmed salmon and Norwegians weren't eating as much as they used to. Because fish sold to be eaten raw fetched a much higher price than fish to be cooked, Norway undertook a marketing campaign to sell their salmon to be eaten raw in Japan. The country established "Project Japan" and sent Bjorn Eirik Olsen to Tokyo in 1986 to head the effort to open the Japanese market to Norway's salmon.

It took a few years, but Olsen sold a huge order of Norwegian salmon to a Japanese frozen foods distributor for a discount steep enough they couldn't say no. But there was a catch: The salmon could only be sold in grocery stores as sushi-grade sashimi. Because the taste and texture was good—and diners didn't get sick—the Norwegian salmon became a hit. In fact, the first sushi chef in Tokyo to try Norwegian salmon, Yutaka Ishinabe, who was famous as one of the Iron Chefs on the first season of that show in 1993, found that it was much fattier than Japanese salmon, perfect for sushi, and his endorsement led to other chefs serving salmon for the first time.

Salmon has been part of sushi in Japan ever since, and with improvements in refrigeration, where deep-freezing wild-caught Pacific salmon can kill off parasites, it's not just Norwegian-farmed Atlantic salmon anymore (still, farmed salmon is the preferred source).

Another surprising Scandinavian contribution to sushi culture is *kazunoko*, the elongated yellow sac of eggs from herring. Because of overfishing, the herring supply was shrinking in Japan, while in Denmark, locally caught herring were thriving. The Danes pickled or cooked their herring but discarded the eggs, which must have seemed like heresy to Japanese. So now the eggs are shipped to Japan (again, thanks to refrigeration and air transport, the byproducts of globalization!) and then cleaned and reshaped in molds into their original kazunoko shape to be used atop nigiri sushi. If you try a kazunoko sushi in the US, check to see if it's an actual egg sac or one that's been molded with imported eggs.

Kazunoko is a pretty specialized sushi ingredient, though. It has a crunchy texture and salty ocean flavor. It's hard to imagine a lot of Americans would order it. Other types of fish eggs are more familiar to Americans, especially the bright orange *ikura*, or salmon roe. Open-mindedness and a sense of culinary adventure are what have made sushi popular—finally—in the West.

Supermarket sushi and beyond

To be fair, sushi was popular in the United States—for a few years—in the late 1800s and early 1900s, when the first Japanophile fad swept through the Western world in the wake of the opening of Japan. Along with racist cultural abominations like Gilbert and Sullivan's *The Mikado* came a wave of sushi served in the few early Japanese restaurants in urban centers like New York and high-society fetes to cater to the early-adopter sophistication of the rich and famous. That's always been the case—hence Michael J. Fox on the cover of *Esquire* and the early embrace of sushi in Hollywood. But with anti-immigrant fervor spreading in the US (the "Gentleman's Agreement" of 1907 prevented immigration of Japanese workers to America except for wives, children, and other family members), sushi's brief time in the limelight faded; by the time World War II broke out, Japanese culture in general was *persona non grata* in the US.

So the fact that sushi is now available at your neighborhood supermarket is a major cultural accomplishment. Not surprisingly, supermarket sushi, in those instantly recognizable rectangular black plastic trays with clear plastic lids, a couple of pieces of plastic "bamboo leaves" as decoration, a glob of wasabi, and a pinch of pink ginger in the corner, caught on first in California.

The first sushi to be served up in a supermarket was way back in 1986 in Marina Del Rey, when a sushi bar opened up in a Vons grocery store. By the 1990s San Diego–area supermarkets regularly had prepackaged sushi. Into the 2000s, sushi began appearing in supermarket deli sections or nearby, at the store's very own dedicated sushi kiosk.

The "Sushi King of Texas," Glen Yoshiaki Gondo, worked in his family's Japanese restaurant in Dallas as a young man, but was catering for Houston-based Continental Airlines when he had the idea to make restaurant-quality sushi for sale in grocery stores. He eventually opened sushi bars in H-E-B supermarkets, first in Houston in 2002 and then throughout the chain in Texas and Mexico. Because of his location, in the grand JA tradition of adaptation, he offers spicy versions of sushi with jalapeno peppers.

Many of the Kroger supermarkets in the Denver area, known locally as King Soopers, have sushi kiosks. They're run by Snowfox, a franchise company owned by Korean entrepreneur Jim Kim, which is the third-largest sushi kiosk provider in the US, with franchises in airports, university campuses, and, of course, grocery stores. Its first location was a sushi bar in a Houston supermarket back in 2005. Now the company runs 1,100 sushi kiosks in thirty-seven states, bringing sushi to the consumers' neighborhood so they don't have to go out to a restaurant for their fix.

The next innovation wending its way across America's Japanese food landscape is *kaiten* sushi, or conveyor-belt sushi restaurants. It has nothing to do with the actual sushi—except in Japan, where some of the big chains already have machines producing sushi in

"Babysat by a Sushi Bar"

. . . .

I grew up in Westport, CT. When my parents split in 1971, when I was fourteen years old, my mom moved into New York City. She was a textile designer and worked in the garment district. Over the years, when my brother and I went to visit her, she'd have to pop into the office for a while. Her office was on the upper floor of a building that had a *kaiten* sushi restaurant on the first floor. She'd park my brother at the conveyor belt and let us grab as many $1+ plates of sushi and other Japanese dishes as we wanted until she came back to get us. . . .

a backroom to be set on the belt for delivery out to the diners. In the US, conveyor belt sushi shops still have sushi chefs standing in the middle of the restaurant, hand-forming nigiri and setting them on dishes that travel the room on the belt. The idea is simple: By delivering sushi around a larger area than just a small bar, the chefs can serve more customers. Is it a little less intimate and not conducive to conversation with the chef? Yes . . . but it's a cool way to have sushi.

Kaiten sushi isn't a modern concept. It was invented in Japan in 1958—it's almost as old as I am!—by Yoshiaki Shiraishi, a sushi restaurant owner in Osaka, who wanted to more efficiently serve his customers and was inspired by beer bottles on an assembly line. By letting customers choose their sushi as it rolled by, his restaurant eliminated the need for servers and made the operation, well, more efficient, like a food factory. By lowering expenses, he was able to lower costs, and his concept became all the rage in Japan. At one point, Shiraishi's Genroku Sangyo chain boasted 240 franchises.

Foreigners were first exposed to kaiten sushi at Shiraishi's restaurant at the Osaka World Expo in 1970.

Some visionary entrepreneurs have taken his lead and opened kaiten sushi shops in the US. Los Angeles's Little Tokyo has had a restaurant for some time. Denver's Sushi-Rama, a spin-off eatery of a local ramen shop, entertains and feeds sushi fans.

One of the better-known chains in Japan serving kaiten sushi, Hanamaru, only has a few locations throughout the country, but its original location was in my mom's hometown of Nemuro, in Hokkaido—where the seafood is about as fresh as you can possibly get. When I went, the fish was excellent, and we kept grabbing plates as they went by. At the end, five of us must have had thirty or more plates of different colors—the color indicated the price. Yet dinner was surprisingly affordable.

The Japanese chain Kura Sushi (which originally spelled its name as "Kula" when they launched here) has made inroads in the United States—you can see many reviews by delighted YouTubers having their fill of sushi, from Texas to California, Washington D,C to Washington state. Kura Sushi borrowed a marketing idea from Japan, where diners get prizes—often cute toys or stickers like something from a Cracker Jack box, only bigger—for eating a certain number of plates. Kura Sushi plans to have one thousand restaurants around the globe by 2030—a lofty target that will certainly bring sushi to even more people everywhere.

. . . At that time, we raised our hands and the waiter would come over, count the plates, and write a check that my mom would pay. None of my CT friends had ever had sushi, not to mention even heard of it. And here we were being babysat by a sushi bar. I remember it was called Genroku Sushi. I didn't realize it was one of the first sushi restaurants in NYC. They even talk about the Americanization of sushi via this place.

Laura Bloom

To do this, modern kaiten sushi chains have developed ever-more complex multi-track systems to deliver both sushi placed at random and on "express-train" tracks, bringing customers sushi ordered from high-tech touchscreen menu at the table.

The downside of all this automated and mass-produced sushi? The rise of conveyor belt restaurants has hurt the small sushi restaurant—the family-owned counters where a master-artisan would prepare and fastidiously assemble sushi by hand.

The 2011 documentary *Jiro Dreams of Sushi* introduced the highest of high-end sushi to American audiences, with shop owner Jiro Ono's twenty-course sushi meals costing almost $300 and requiring reservations months in advance. In Japan, such an exclusive, traditional sushi experience can probably survive even as the industry evolves around it and automates both the making and serving of sushi. For Americans who want fast gratification at the lowest prices, though, the conveyor belt model might win out in the end.

6 Oodles of Noodles

Udon, Soba, and Ramen

I have vivid childhood memories of noodles in Japan. I can still see bowls of ramen and lacquer boxes of soba noodles stacked precariously high in trays or boxes, being delivered by men riding bicycles through crazy Tokyo traffic. The deliverymen (they were always men when I was a kid in early 1960s Tokyo) might wobble from time to time with their trays perched on their shoulders, but their elbows and necks would adjust to bumps like human shock absorbers, and they always made it to their destinations to feed hungry salarymen at nearby offices.

My mom didn't make ramen at home, but we did eat soba, especially in the summer, when my mom would make the salty shoyu-and-dashi dipping sauce that we would dunk strands of brownish buckwheat noodles into before slurping them up. Ramen was reserved for meals out at *ramen-ya*, a ramen shop, which specialized in the dish. My mom, it turns out, preferred soba or the fat, white udon noodles to the yellowish ramen ones, and considered ramen "Chinese food"—said, sadly, with some derision. But dang, the rest of the world, including Japan and America, loves ramen.

Ramen's roots were indeed in China. It had been around since the late 1800s in Japan, but it was during the post–World War II years, and particularly in the 1960s, when ramen became the ubiquitous Japanese comfort food it is today.

I loved ramen as a child, and when my family moved to the States in the mid-sixties I was sad to find that ramen wasn't sold in the few Japanese restaurants that were available here. But in 1970 Nissin, the company that invented instant ramen in 1958, began selling it in the US. The next year, the company rolled out Cup Noodles.

A lot of Americans have memories of ramen too, but mostly of the cheap instant ramen boiled in a pot of water with small packets of flavoring and condiments sprinkled in.

Several generations of college students have grown up with instant ramen and Cup Noodles since the seventies. Who can argue when each savory serving can cost just pennies? Lots of people even use instant ramen as a base for fancier dishes by adding meats and vegetables. But I think that's cheating. We'll get back to the instant stuff later, but if you want to have some "real" ramen, nothing beats going to a good ramen-ya for a bowl.

A brief history of ramen

A steaming bowl of fresh ramen is salty and meaty with hints of chicken, pork, and fish bathing together like it's a friendly hot tub of flavor. The noodles are firm and chewy (though a good ramen-ya will offer the option to have your noodles hard or soft to your liking) with just the right amount of absorption of the soup, and the toppings can be creative but respect tradition. The experience is several cuts above plopping a square of fried, dried noodles into a saucepan for a few minutes or pouring boiling water into the Styrofoam cup and waiting two minutes with the top flap closed (no peeking!). Instant ramen is cheap, but it's not food for the soul. The noodles go immediately limp, the soup is flavored hot water (though it can fool your brain into thinking you just ate some real food), and out of the box, the toppings are . . . well, there are no actual toppings, just some dehydrated little vegetable bits.

"I Never Thought I'd See"

. . . .

You can tell Japanese food has become Americanized because of sushi everywhere. I never thought I'd see the day when a permanent wooden sushi sign adorned the back wall of our local Kroger store or oodles of instant Japanese noodles available at places like Costco, whether it's udon (ooh-dohn) or *tonkotsu* (not to be confused with *tonkatsu*) ramen. You see packaged, seasoned nori in general markets and so many types of matcha-flavored drinks and food.

Erin Yoshimura

Ramen's origins are in the hand-pulled Chinese noodles called *lamian*. The noodles in soup were originally sold at Chinese food carts and restaurants in Japanese port cities during the late 1800s and early 1900s, as working-class food for Chinese laborers and students. The first Chinese restaurant opened in Yokohama (where a thriving Chinatown still exists) in 1870, and later, lamian evolved into the Japanese dish. The first ramen restaurant, Rairaiken, opened in Tokyo's Asakusa district in 1910.

It's also important to keep in mind that when it comes to Japanese cuisine, ramen is not the be-all and end-all of noodles. Japan has a long association with noodles that goes back hundreds of years before ramen arrived. Soba, traditionally made from buckwheat, and udon, made from wheat flour, are both older and a more established part of Japan's food culture. However, like ramen, both udon and soba probably came from China around the eighth century. Udon became popular throughout Japan in the 1600s and soba in the 1700s. These noodles no doubt had a big impact on the later development of ramen. What makes ramen noodles distinct from other wheat noodles? Ramen noodles are alkaline, that is, they are less acidic. The addition of *kansui*, an alkaline mineral solution, to the dough gives the noodles both their yellowish color and chewy texture.

Ramen is a Japanese cultural institution. Different cities and regions have developed unique ramen styles and enhancements. Sapporo is famous for miso ramen, Hakodate for *shio* (salt), Tokyo for shoyu. Hakata *tonkotsu* ramen, everyone's current favorite, is a rich pork-bone broth that simmers the bones so long that the ramen has a layer of fatty collagen on top. There's also an Okinawan variation, Okinawa soba, which features fatter ramen noodles that look like udon.

You can't beat ramen in Japan. One of the best I ever had was a decade ago in a tiny hole-in-the-wall in Kyoto, Dai Ichi Asahi, just a couple blocks from the Japan Rail station. They served their rich, porky soup and thin, straight noodles topped off with huge handfuls of *naga negi*, a long green onion, and *moyashi*, bean sprouts.

That was wonderful. When I was in Kumamoto in Kyushu, we had the absolute best ramen I've ever had, in a tiny family-owned place that relatives took us to, and I regret I didn't note the name of the shop. Having super-rich, creamy tonkotsu in the region where the style was invented was an amazing experience. We ate in a tiny, unassuming place but the ramen was incredible.

We've also had the opportunity to visit the Shin-Yokohama Ramen Museum south of Tokyo. It's a crazy re-creation of a Tokyo neighborhood circa 1958, not coincidentally, the year instant ramen was introduced. I was born in Tokyo in 1957, so the museum captures my childhood memories of the city, with grimy buildings, old-school phone booths, period billboards, and electrical and telephone wires crisscrossing between buildings above the streets and alleys, all forever preserved in a dusky twilight. The museum isn't just for show—it features some of the best and best-known ramen shops from all across Japan, serving small bowls of their local specialty.

The museum is a reflection of Japan's reverence for ramen as a cultural heritage (even if it was originally imported); nearby in Yokohama there's also a museum dedicated to the technological innovation of instant ramen.

The ramen craze in America

Real ramen has caught on in the US too, but more so in urban centers where Japanese and other Asian immigrant communities live and eat. But in middle America, including Denver, real ramen is still somewhat of a novelty. Some Japanese restaurants might serve ramen, but it takes a lot of time and dedication to make it right. So most Japanese restaurants will stick to the reliable standards like teriyaki and sushi. A few Japanese restaurants here serve pretty good ramen, but honestly, the best ramen is served at places that specialize in only ramen, where the soup stock can be simmered all day to get it just right. Denver now has several restaurants that do that, and one even makes its noodles daily in house.

If you're lucky, you live in a city where ramen has always been part of the culinary scene, or where the ramen fad has already caught on fire, like New York, Seattle, San Francisco, or Los Angeles.

Too many restaurants across the US don't specialize in the dish, or are run by people who aren't serious rameniacs, but are only looking to ride the coattails of a fad. The noodles are never quite right, the soup can taste like dishwater, and the ingredients simply are obscene . . . really, broccoli atop a bowl of ramen? Or the ramen noodles are served in what tastes like udon stock broth made with katsuobushi. Yuck. Fine for udon, but don't try to bamboozle us by tossing in different noodles and calling it ramen.

In California, a personal fave in San Francisco's Japantown, Iroha, close,d but it has been replaced by a very good chain from Southern California, Ramen Yamadaya. I also always visit a couple other shops in San Francisco's J-Town: the tiny (and often very busy) Suzu Noodle House and Tanpopo, beneath Yamadaya, which has been there for a long time.

Los Angeles has a bunch of great ramen places, many of which have opened in the past few years. Some are overrated and filled with hipsters who don't know better—I'm mystified as to why they're so popular. In LA's Little Tokyo, Daikokuya, with its yellow awning, always has lines outside. But look closer and you'll see very few Asians in line and even fewer Japanese. Not that Asians are the arbiters of quality or even authenticity, but the crowds in that place don't know any better.

The food there is okay, but just a few doors down is a place I've liked much better for years, San Sui Tei, which was owned by a Chinese man who ran a ramen shop in Japan before coming to LA. The service could get bogged down when he was busy (it was just him and a few helpers), but the fried rice was heavenly and the tonkotsu broth was rich and savory. The experience was just nicer than Daikokuya, where you feel rushed because there are twenty people outside waiting for your seat.

San Sui Tei closed even before the Coronavirus pandemic, but since then other shops have sprung up around the Little Tokyo neighborhood, and elsewhere. Now I have a new favorite place for ramen in LA's Little Tokyo. On a recommendation from a Japanese friend in Denver, I tried Men Oh, which opened in 2012 in a strip mall a couple of blocks from Daikokuya and San Sui Tei (in Honda Plaza, the same place as my favorite Hawaiian breakfast joint, Aloha Cafe!). I had their specialty, Tokushima black-garlic ramen, with gyoza and it was amazing. Really. It rocked my world.

That same trip, I also had a very good tonkotsu ramen at Ramen Yamadaya in Torrance, an LA suburb (you can find photos of a lot of these meals on my Instagram). It's one of the locations of the same California chain that I enjoyed in San Francisco. And I've had good ramen—or rather, ramen that I liked—at other places around LA, including Shin Sen Gumi (a chain I first enjoyed inside a Marukai Market) and Orochon, which has a silly challenge as a gimmick. If you can eat a 2.2-pound bowl of their extra spicy ramen in thirty minutes, you get a t-shirt and your photo on their wall (but you still have to pay for your ramen).

RAMEN, THE "IT" FOOD: (*above*) Although ramen is the hip new thing in America, soba has an even longer history in Japan. Traditionally made of buckwheat, it's often served in a lacquer box with dipping sauce on the side. (*top right*) The Shin-Yokohama Ramen Museum features a recreation of Tokyo in the 1950s and serves all sorts of styles of ramen for you to try. (*bottom right*) A selection of instant ramen noodles. Not as good as the genuine article but will do in a pinch. And it sure is convenient.

You can also find delicious reliable ramen if you live near a Mitsuwa Marketplace, because most of them have a Santouka ramen-ya in their food court. I've had Santouka, a popular chain from Japan, in New Jersey and San Diego, and it's pretty great.

But now that ramen's catching on stateside, beware the rise of hipster noodle joints. On earlier LA trips, I've tried Tsujita, a super-trendy place in the already-trendy Sawtelle Japanese district. The place is famous for tsukemen, in which noodles are served separate from a bowl of concentrated dipping soup, and for its tonkotsu ramen. I'm not a big fan of tsukemen—I like my noodles swimming in hot soup—and I don't care for Tsujita's tonkotsu. It's too fatty, and I felt like I'd been French kissing a can of Crisco shortening after I had the ramen.

One person's greasy kiss is another's orgasmic foodie experience, though. A lot of people like Tsujita and, yes, Daikokuya. Ramen is truly a subjective, individual taste. For all I know, some of the ramen that I think are awful might taste great to someone from Japan. I don't think so, but it's possible. I may not like them all, but at least in LA I have the choice of many recommended places for ramen!

I have yet to noodle around the East Coast ramen scene, but one place I do want to try next time I make it to New York is Ivan Ramen, a shop with a non-Japanese pedigree that was minted in Tokyo and now has an international reputation. Ivan Orkin was born in Long Island and started his food career as a dishwasher in a sushi restaurant. He studied Japanese at the University of Colorado in Boulder, then went to Japan to teach English right out of college. He returned to the US in 1990 and attended the Culinary Institute of America, then worked in various restaurant and food industry positions until going back to Japan. In 2006 he made the bold move of opening Ivan Ramen in Tokyo, brave because ramen by then was such a Japanese cultural tradition that it was difficult to see Tokyoites embracing a gaijin feeding them quality noodles and soup. But he did, and his restaurant was a hit. He opened a second location in Tokyo but returned to his roots in New York, opening a ramen shop in Manhattan in 2013. He then opened his world-famous Ivan Ramen in the Lower East Side.

By then, ramen had already become an "It" food, the Next Big Thing. Celebrity chef David Chang helped spark the craze in 2004 when he opened Momofuku Noodle Bar in New York City. Ironically, he named it after Momofuku Ando, the man who invented both instant ramen and Cup Noodles, but his artisan ramen bowls were anything but cheapo college-student fare, and his East Village locale was a perfect destination for hipsters who crowned him the reigning king of ramen. Along with the explosion of Japanese chains opening up on the West Coast and, less than a decade later, the arrival of Ivan Ramen, the humble Japanese noodle bowl, the source of sustenance for zillions of workaday Japanese salarymen and women, who often ate standing in ramen stalls the size of American closets, became elevated to the classy, trendy cuisine we seek out today.

In comparison, for years Denver was a dry, barren desert for ramen lovers.

Not long ago only a couple of places served the stuff, including one, a lonely American branch of the Japanese Oshima Ramen chain that was too far ahead of its time. When it opened in 2000 it was the only place serving ramen in Denver—hell, probably anywhere in Colorado. It started promisingly, though the bowls were too expensive for the time. The noodles were housemade with flour flown in from Japan, and the broth was carefully simmered and lovingly nurtured. But the original owner sold the place, and in the ensuing years it deteriorated into a dirty eatery serving second-rate soup and what tasted like characterless store-bought noodles. Oshima finally gave up the ghost in 2014 just as a new generation of real ramen restaurants began simmering on the local culinary scene.

I first wrote optimistically in 2009 about the emerging scene. Of the places I mentioned in 2009, most are already gone. Bento Zanmai in Boulder and Taki's in Denver are both long closed. Likewise Happy Noodle House, a trendy shop opened by serial Boulder restaurateur David Query (nope, not Asian), which shut as soon as he thought the fad was over. Frank Bonanno's pan-Asian Denver bistro, Bones, served their lovely Lobster Ramen for a good run, but it was pricey and only for special occasions, not a standby comfort food. Okole Maluna ("bottoms up" in Hawaiian), a Hawaiian restaurant north of Denver in the small town of Windsor, served the Hawaiian-style ramen called saimin, which of course had slivers of Spam on top of the noodles. But during the economic crunch of the pandemic, Okole Maluna, like many other restaurants across the country, shut down. We still miss it.

Denver does now have several new and legitimate ramen-ya—places that focus on ramen as their primary mission. My current local ramen-ya faves are Tokio in downtown Denver and Ramen Star, where the owner makes his noodles daily before opening the restaurant. Another hot spot, Osaka Ramen, uses local ingredients like Olathe sweet corn in the summer (an ingredient that's common in ramen from Sapporo), and in the fall, a spicy blend of freshly harvested green chiles and Mexican chorizo sausage. Tokio has a "Cremoso Diablo" ramen on its menu, which adds spicy peppers to a broth enriched with cheese. Yes, cheese. Another Denver shop with several locations, Sukiya, adds tomato paste to its popular Fukuoka-style pork ramen and calls it "Bloody Mary Tonkotsu." Although you might find tomato or cheese added to bowls of ramen in some adventurous shops in Japan, these are not traditional recipes, that's for sure!

Traditional or contemporary, the future looks bright for Colorado's ramen lovers. But even if the scene cools down, I'll always find great ramen on the coasts . . . and I never turn down a chance to have ramen when I'm in Japan!

Ramen, fast and slow

Ramen's arrival in trendy US restaurants was really a slow creep until some established Japanese chains crossed the Pacific to open satellites here and some brave name-brand chefs opened their high-profile eateries. David Chang is a well-known food auteur today, with a string of Netflix mini-documentary series about his culinary explorations. He focuses on not just ramen but Japanese food in general—one fascinating episode showed how bonito, or skipjack tuna, is fermented and smoked into the petrified pieces that are shaved into katsuobushi, the lifeblood of Japanese dashi soup.

But when he first made a splash with his Manhattan ramen shop, Momofuku Noodle Bar, Chang paid honest tribute to the depth of appreciation American have had for ramen for decades, long before the $15 bowl of tonkotsu became a familiar site on Yelp. It's right there in the name.

Momofuku Ando's invention of instant ramen in the late 1950s, and then Cup Noodles in the 1970s, changed the way Japanese ate ramen because of its heartiness and convenience, perfect for a modern lifestyle and changing family dynamics.

In the United States, instant ramen was maybe envisioned like frozen dinners and canned food for family meals, but instead it became an indispensable staple of college students across America. That's because instant ramen was super cheap and super easy to make, especially since it came in its own Styrofoam cup and didn't even need a pot to mix it in.

And like the revolution of real ramen in the US, the instant ramen revolution in Japan took some time to take hold.

Momofuku Ando, who started out his business career selling textiles, saw a need to help feed people in postwar Japan. In response to a food shortage crisis exacerbated by the devastation of World War II, the American Occupation government was pushing Japanese to use surplus wheat flour from the US to make bread. Ando, who was born in Taiwan (then Japanese-controlled Formosa) and moved to Japan in 1933 to study at university and start a clothing company in Osaka, wondered why there was so much emphasis on using the flour for bread when historically the Japanese used wheat for noodles (udon especially, but buckwheat was used for soba).

Since Chinese introduced ramen to Japan starting in port cities like Yokohama, ramen noodles were called "*Shina soba*," or Chinese noodles. My mom has called ramen Shina soba, because that's what it was called when she was young. Ramen was better known to the Japanese by World War II, and in the postwar years, Ando thought noodles made with the surplus American wheat would make cost-effective, nutritious food. Noodles of any kind would be more familiar to Japanese than the Western emphasis on bread. His idea was to dehydrate manufactured, pre-cooked noodles and then rehydrate them for a quick and easy meal. So he went about experimenting with ways to flash-fry noodles that could be reconstituted in boiling water and retain the original texture and flavor of fresh noodles.

After perfecting the process, he launched his noodles as "Chikin Ramen" in 1958, made by his company, Nissin, which today is the giant of the packaged-ramen industry. It's also now spelled Chicken Ramen. Each block of dried ramen was already infused with the soup flavoring, but later the noodles came with a packet of seasoning to add to the boiling water. I grew up with this type of ramen as a kid in Japan. My mom wasn't in the habit of making ramen for meals, but she considered this an acceptable food for us to have as a snack, I guess.

When it was first sold, Nissin's Chikin Ramen cost ¥35—mere pennies, but a higher price than fresh noodles at the time. It took some time before Japanese consumers began buying the instant

"My Latest Experiments"

. . . .

My latest experiments have been to sate my wife's and our roommate's cravings for ramen. One of our favorite ramen restaurants, Noraneko, closed permanently due to the pandemic, so I've been doing my best to replicate some of the flavors you get from good ramen spots. As a lifelong picky eater, I have become accustomed to taking what I want from one recipe and mashing it together with another, and using what we had on hand in the pantry and fridge. So I took this approach to make homemade *shoyu* ramen.

Cay Fletcher

stuff for its convenience. It was a mainstay in Japan by the 1970s, when Nissin began selling its Top Ramen brand in the United States. Ramen caught on but needed an evolutionary push to become mainstream.

That's when Ando realized the cultural differences between Japan and America. He noticed that when Americans made Top Ramen, if there wasn't a saucepan handy, they would break up the noodles and drop them into a mug and add hot water. Since people in the US didn't all have the size and type of bowls that typically accommodate ramen, and didn't normally use chopsticks, Ando decided to make it a snap for Americans to enjoy his ramen. He formed his dried noodles to fit into a Styrofoam cup and added the seasoning for soup into the cup beneath the dried disk of noodles.

When Cup Noodles was invented and hit the shelves in 1971, it became easier than ever to prepare a satisfying, hot serving of ramen—just pour in boiling water and fold down the thin lid over the Styrofoam lip for a couple of minutes, then peel back the lid and eat away.

No wonder then that college students glommed onto ramen as the inexpensive food of choice to go with both studying and partying. Even as recently as the 2000s, a packet of instant ramen or a cup of noodles cost just a few dimes. Once microwaves became dorm room equipment, it was a no-brainer to heat up water for your ramen fix. Intrepid Japanese American students went a step further and heated up their ramen in the small-sized rice cooker their parents bought for them to take to school.

Instant ramen is sold these days in almost every American supermarket chain—Nissin (the company that Ando launched) and Maruchan are the best-known Japanese brands, with both their square packages of instant noodles in several flavors and the cup-noodle variety lined up on the shelves of the "Asian foods" aisle. But there's a bewildering array of instant ramen now available at any Asian supermarket, including the popular Korean American–owned chain H Mart as well as local Chinese and Japanese groceries. You'll see not just Japanese packages of instant ramen, but also Korean, Vietnamese, Chinese, Filipino, and Thai brands.

Ramen's island cousin, Saimin was first cooked up in the nineteenth and early-twentieth century during Hawaii's plantation boom, when Chinese, Japanese, Korean, Filipino, and Portuguese immigrants arrived as laborers for the islands' sugar cane and pineapple plantations. Saimin is a uniquely Hawaiian noodle served in hot soup, with toppings that would look familiar to any fan of ramen or Okinawan soba: green onions, chashu, kamaboko, nori, or egg. As noted earlier, we still miss the saimin served by the now-closed Okole Maluna in Northern Colorado.

After becoming a bit passe in Hawaii in recent years, saimin is enjoying a resurgence, thanks to the support of Sun Noodles, the Hawaii-based manufacturer and supplier of fresh packaged noodles, including ramen, to the best restaurants across the US. Sun sponsors an annual noodle festival that promotes saimin as the homegrown star, and the amazing Hawaiian restaurant chain Zippy's has always had saimin on its menu, selling almost a million bowls in 2018. The chain is planning an outpost in Las Vegas, so it shouldn't take long before the rest of America catches on to Hawaii's secret cousin to ramen.

Bowl Me Over
Anything on a Bowl of Rice Is Delicious

Rice is undoubtedly the foundation of Japanese cuisine. It's hard to imagine living in Japan or dining at a Japanese restaurant in the US without rice. Let's be clear though: We're not talking Uncle Ben's or Rice-A-Roni. Nor are we referring to jasmine rice, a standard in Chinese fare. Japanese rice is uniquely fluffy and sticky at the same time—ideal for picking up with chopsticks. Rice in Japan is a staple that's been grown for two thousand years. Yet it only became commonly eaten by all people, instead of just the upper classes, in the eighteenth century, and it took until the twentieth century before rice became the all-important foundation of Japanese food.

In Japan, rice has a long history that included being used as a form of currency (to pay taxes, for instance), for use in ceremonial rituals, and as a part of holiday celebrations. The rice grain can be found in multiple variations, which range from the most common and prized white rice, with all the husk, germ, and bran polished off, to brown rice, with only the husk removed but the bran and germ left unpolished, making it the healthier choice.

There is more than one variety of rice used in Japan. *Mochigome*, or glutinous sticky rice, is used to make mochi, which Americans have come to love as the chewy exterior of mochi ice cream and which Oshogatsu wouldn't be the same without. Regular short-grain Japanese rice is sticky but not like mochi rice. It's just sticky enough to make it easy to pick up in lumps or push out from bowls with chopsticks. It's also used to make sake, but we'll come back to that later.

And every part of the rice plant is used in some form or another. After the fall harvest you can drive through rural Japan and see columns of smoke from the burning of rice husks, but the stalks are used to make tatami mats, sandals, and sacred rope—the thick traditional ceremonial rope at the entrance of shrines and temples.

There is nothing so heartwarming to Japanese or Japanese Americans as a bowl of freshly cooked, steaming rice waiting for the accompaniments that will make it a meal. In Japan, rice is considered the soul of a meal, with the rest of the food served on small plates or bowls around it. For a traditional *teishoku*, or "set meal," served in a restaurant or at a Japanese home, the dishes would be arranged with the rice in front left (the most important and first position) as the diner faces the meal, with soup on the right, a protein like meat or fish in the back, and vegetables and tsukemono as a side dish.

Not all meals are so strictly structured, of course.

Donburi

Because it's always served with meals, rice also became the base
ingredient for popular *donburi*, a large bowl of rice topped with
meat and vegetables, which usually surround the rice in small
dishes for a set meal. The donburi, which refers to the bowl itself
as well as the meal, is about the size of a ramen bowl. It can be
cheap and easy to make, and therefore donburi meals are popular
with home cooks on the go and at restaurants that serve workers
looking for a quick lunch. You can top a bowl of rice with just about
anything in the Japanese culinary canon.

Let's take *gyudon* for example.

Gyu means beef in Japanese, and *don* is a shortened form of
donburi. Simple! Therefore, other types of donburi are easy to fig-
ure out: *Tendon* is tempura served over a bowl of rice; *katsudon* is
tonkatsu served atop rice (with a savory sauce and slightly cooked
eggs); *oyakodon* is "parent-and-child donburi," made with chicken
and eggs simmered in a savory sauce and, you guessed it, served
over rice.

Gyudon is the oldest of the donburi and was first served during
the Meiji period in the late 1800s, when the emperor proclaimed
that meat was approved for eating by the general public. For several hundred years before, Buddhist religious beliefs limited most
meat for most Japanese. One reason for the change in diet was the
government's concern that Japanese needed to become bigger and
stronger to compete with the "barbarian" Americans, who had
recently arrived in the country. To become a modern nation, Japan
needed modern citizens, not just modern industry.

Unfortunately, in those early decades when meat began being
served, restaurants found that many Japanese, who were not used

to cooking any kind of meat, were put off by the smell. One reason that familiar ingredients like soy sauce, sugar, mirin, and sake were used to marinate meat was to make it palatable to diners. And one of the first meat dishes to catch on was called *gyunabe*, or beef hotpot, made with beef and onions. The original gyunabe sold in a Tokyo restaurant in 1867 used miso to flavor the dish, and the seasoning over time became the sweeter combination of soy sauce and sugar.

With the new sauce, gyunabe began catching on at other restaurants, and thanks to the addition of more vegetables and ingredients like tofu, the dish eventually evolved by the 1890s into what we know today as sukiyaki. The name may have come from the use of spades by farmers to grill their food over a fire, but the ingredients came from gyunabe. Meanwhile, observant restaurant owners saw that some customers poured the leftover soup from their gyudon over bowls of rice to get every last drop of deliciousness. Besides, gyunabe was expensive by Japanese dining standards of the time, and nobody liked to waste their food.

There was an opportunity to save money (and serve more customers) by using fewer ingredients and serving them in a donburi filled with rice. So along with sukiyaki, the prototype gyunabe also led to gyudon.

In 1899, the name many people today associate immediately with beef bowls was established. Yoshinoya was founded by Eikichi Matsuda in Tokyo, who perfected the process of serving gyudon. The company's expansion has been relentless, and Yoshinoya now operates over one thousand restaurants around the world, including over one hundred in the United States. All of them are currently in California, although they've had locations in the past in Nevada, Texas, New York, and Colorado.

In fact, Yoshinoya established its first office outside Japan in Denver, Colorado, in 1973 to export American beef to Japan, and opened the first Yoshinoya restaurant in Denver in 1975. My younger brother worked at the first location near downtown Denver when he was still in high school. There were several locations in the area, but the company eventually pulled out of Colorado. However, one of its executives, Mareo Torito, stayed and took over a couple of Denver-area locations, opening them as Kokoro ("Heart"). Over the decades, Torito has diversified and now runs an organic chicken company called Redbird, and his son Masaru manages the Kokoro restaurants as pioneering fast-casual Japanese eateries—one even has drive-through ordering and pickup.

The menu still features beef bowls, and they taste the same as they did years ago (just like Japan's Yoshinoya locations). But Kokoro now also sells an interesting mix of Japanese cuisine served up fast and casual: donburi topped with grilled salmon, chicken, or beef; chicken donburi with curry sauce; *unagi*, grilled freshwater eel over rice (something that Yoshinoya sells in Japan); tendon with shrimp tempura; several types of ramen; and some noodle dishes named for the American customers, like "Splash" (pretty authentic udon, also available topped with shrimp tempura) and "Sobaghetti" (yakisoba). Kokoro also serves a variety of sushi, soups, and salads. But the beef bowls are what the restaurants are still known for the best: tasty, thin-sliced beef simmered with onions in a sweet marinade and scooped atop a bowl of perfectly cooked white rice.

What could be more Japanese than that? There's more than one hundred and fifty years of gyudon history in each bowl.

More foods over rice

It's not surprising that other restaurants in many cities serve up their versions of beef bowls. And one Colorado chain that's obviously based on the Yoshinoya/Kokoro fast-casual concept currently has forty-six locations throughout Denver as well as in Arizona and Texas.

Tokyo Joe's pays tribute to its Japanese inspiration in its name, which is also the title of a 1949 film starring Humphrey Bogart, set during the US Occupation of Japan. The chain was founded in 1996 by a former professional skier Larry Leith to serve food that was decidedly more American than Japanese, with a menu that included many fusion variants. One called "Mojoe" has dark-meat chicken, pineapple, eggs, and vegetables in a "sweet & tangy" sauce and served over rice. Another of its signature bowls, "BBQ Banh Mi," is a cultural mashup that can make your head spin.

Early on, Tokyo Joe's claimed its food was "Japanese inspired." Now it doesn't mention its inspiration. Such is the popularity of Japanese bowls in a globalized food chain—authenticity is sometimes shunted aside for the sake of audience.

There are more productive ways of bridging cultures. Old-school, Japanese-owned Chinese restaurants used to serve their version of Chinese food. In the past, Chinese were raised not to mix their food with the rice, because the rice would absorb the flavor and dissipate it too quickly. So, although there are lots of classic Chinese dishes, if you think about it, not many are served with the entree poured over the rice. They might be served side by side or in a separate bowl or dish.

Japanese don't hesitate to put their dishes over rice if it needs to be served that way, including Japanese cooking Chinese food. *Machi chuka* ("City Chinese") is an old-fashioned term that was used to describe a neighborhood Chinese restaurant, a type of business that's disappearing in modern Japan as conveyor-belt sushi and hip ramen shops proliferate. But for older diners, machi chuka food brings back memories of comfort food from decades ago.

One Denver Japanese restaurant, Sakura House, serves home-style Japanese dishes and bowls of ramen, but the couple who run it have added some machi chuka specialties, including an *umani yakisoba*, which has noodles with pork and vegetables in a thick gravy made of potato starch typical of Chinese resturants. Making the gravy thicker than just a sauce made it possible to pour Sakura House's machi chuka dishes over rice without immediately making the rice soggy. The owner told me that he and his wife serve these dishes because they're popular with older Japanese customers, who marvel at the memories the food recalls of their younger days in Japan.

*

Sakura House also serves another dish over rice that's one of the most-loved dishes in Japan: curry.

In fact, *kareraisu* (curry rice) is the number-one most popular dish in Japan—most Japanese have it at least once a week. Families look forward to having it, and mothers who usually do the cooking love that it's quick and easy to make. They can find it in many restaurants, including chains that sell only various curry dishes, with varying levels of spiciness. That's a staggering number of people having curry.

Curry, which is an Anglicized version of the Tamil word for "sauce," was brought to Japan by the Royal British Navy during the

Meiji period, and the Japanese navy saw that the dish seemed to prevent beriberi, a disease caused by a deficiency of the vitamin thiamine. All the nutrients were polished out of white rice in the Japanese diet, but the meat and flour used to thicken the gravy had plenty of thiamine. The British had created a powdered curry mix so it was easy to cook up curry on the high seas.

The naval curry was made thick so it wouldn't slosh around in rough waters. The Japanese adopted the curry powder and in typical fashion began making it more to the Japanese liking—the Japanese version is usually sweeter and milder. Because mass amounts could be made to feed many sailors and soldiers quickly and economically, curry became standard military fare. Even today it's served every Friday for dinner by the Maritime Self-Defense Force, the Japanese navy. It wasn't adopted right away by the public because access to the curry powder was reserved for the military and the country's elites, who were embracing Western imports. Still, an early recipe for curry was published in 1872, and by the end of the decade, some Japanese restaurants began adding it to their menus.

A Japanese company, House Foods, developed instant curry roux in powder form in 1926. House Foods is still one of the major brands for curry in Japan. In 1956, another company that's still around and is dominant in Japan, S&B Foods, introduced the game changer of instant-curry roux blocks. Without even needing to measure out the seasoning, home chefs could just pop a cube of roux from the box into the pot, and *voila*—curry! More recently, the industry introduced vacuum-sealed curry gravy that just needs to be heated in boiling water or the microwave. They're so popular that 1,500 different kinds of precooked boil-in-pouch curries are sold in Japan. You want pink-colored curry that's made with beets? It's available, and you just have to heat it up.

ANYTHING AND EVERYTHING OVER RICE: (*top left*) *Umani* yakisoba, Japanese yakisoba with a flavorful gravy reminiscent of Chinese American fare, being cooked to order at Sakura House in Denver. The thick gravy is ideal with rice. (*bottom left*) A treat that not many Americans will have the inclination to try, *tamago kake gohan*, a raw egg mixed into hot rice with soy sauce to season. (*above*) The iconic Hawaiian dish loco moco. It might be served on a plate, not a *donburi*, but it certainly counts as one of the great over-rice dishes.

Curry has been incorporated into all sorts of other foods as well, including ramen, where curry is used to enhance and thicken the soup. Traditionally the thicker udon noodles are used, but there's also curry-flavored instant ramen. An episode of *Midnight Diner: Tokyo Stories,* a series available on Netflix, even had Master, the chef and owner of a tiny diner, make instant ramen and then add curry as a topping. To round it all out, there are lots of curry-flavored snacks, including chips, and a wonderful street-food variation, *karepan,* or curry bread, that we'll dive into in the next chapter.

And even more foods over rice

As you know by now, you can put anything on a bowl of rice and it will be amazing. There's a bowl-ier version of chirashizushi, which isn't always served in a bowl. *Kaisendon* is a sashimi bowl. You'll recognize the "-don" suffix that we mentioned before. *Kaisen* means "seafood," and that's exactly what you get with a kaisendon—seafood on top of a bowl of rice. That's regular white rice, not vinegared sushi rice, which is what makes this different from chirashi. You can find kaisendon in many places around Japan, especially around fish markets and ports. Hokkaido, famous for its fresh seafood, is known for its kaisendon, which can be topped off with the seafood of your choice. Salmon, tuna, and other fish are easy choices. But you can also add slices of abalone, or a spread of bright orange ikura, *uni* (sea urchin), or *hotate* (scallops). Or squid, octopus, and, yes, crab. Heaven for seafood lovers!

Nori tsukudani is a dark-colored paste made of nori seaweed and shoyu. It's available in small jars in many brand names at any Japanese or Asian supermarket. It doesn't look particularly appetizing—it looks like something you might scrape off the bottom of a sewer worker's boots—but it's truly delicious when smeared into hot rice.

Tamago kake gohan is probably something a Westerner would think twice about eating, but I grew up with it and still have it for breakfast from time to time. It's a raw egg and shoyu, mixed together with chopsticks (or a spoon) and then drizzled over a steaming bowl of rice. Yes, raw egg. I put lots of shoyu in the egg so I get the blast of salty umami, and I also shake furikake on top to add more salty seasoning. The rice has to be hot, that's the most important thing. I love the flavor of the egg and soft texture of the rice. In Japan, where eggs are strictly monitored to government health standards, it's common to eat raw eggs, not only over rice but also with sukiyaki, to dip your meats and vegetables in before you eat them, or as a topping on gyudon (which, remember, is a spinoff of sukiyaki) or oyakodon. Standards aren't the same in the US, but I still enjoy raw egg and shoyu over hot rice. When I'm in Japan, I look forward to hotels' breakfast buffets, where I know I'll find a bowl of eggs next to the rice cooker so I can crack one open.

Also at Japanese hotels, I know I'll find another favorite for breakfast, but it's something that I don't expect Americans will ever get used to eating stateside. It's *natto*, fermented soy beans. I love to mix natto with shoyu into hot rice. I even will add natto to my tamago kake gohan. It's an admittedly acquired taste—not even all Japanese like it. But I grew up with it, and I keep little packets of natto in my freezer today. I'll return to natto in the final chapter, on my list of Japanese foods that I know will never ever catch on in the US.

✳

There are three Hawaiian rice dishes worth noting here: *poke*, Zippy's Chili, and loco moco.

Poke (pronounced "poh-kay") is the Hawaiian specialty that qualifies as an island version of a sashimi bowl: Traditional Hawaiian poke is marinated raw fish that's been diced and seasoned with salt, seaweed, and Hawaiian candlenut. It was a great way to use the odd-sized and -shaped scraps from slicing fish for sashimi or sushi. In the past decade, restaurants serving poke in the US mainland exploded. Although our family has had homemade poke with shoyu, sesame oil, and other seasonings, some of the new wave of poke providers add typically American ingredients like avocado, mushrooms, pickled jalapeno peppers, sriracha sauce, and more. Of course, poke should be served over a bowl of rice.

Poke is available everywhere in Hawaii, and increasingly mainland Japanese restaurants are serving poke. You can buy it at shops in Hawaii, and if you're lucky it might even be available in Costco stores. When we were in Oahu a few years back, we were amazed and giddy to see multiple types of poke available in bulk. And the Costco stores even in Colorado have sometimes stocked fresh poke. What a treat!

Loco moco is usually served on a plate: It's rice topped with a hamburger patty and smothered in gravy and one or two fried eggs, like a snowcapped mountain peak. But it can be served in a bowl (the gravy can get messy) and the history of the dish indicates it might have originally been served that way. One version of the origin story is that, in 1949, some students in Hilo, on the Big Island, Hawaii, asked the owners of a restaurant to come up with something they could eat that would be quick, easy, and cheap and wasn't a typical sandwich. They got a burger on rice in a bowl, smothered with gravy, named loco moco after one of the teenagers' friends whose nickname was "Crazy." The fried egg was added to the recipe later. The dish has crossed the Pacific and is available at Hawaiian restaurants like the Aloha Cafe in Los Angeles's Little Tokyo and chains like L&L Hawaiian Barbecue.

Zippy's is a fabulous Hawaiian diner chain that's open twenty-four hours, like a version of Denny's that's zapped with island culture, serving food from Hawaii, Japan, Korea, China, Okinawa, and the mainland. The first Zippy's diner was opened by Japanese American brothers Francis and Charles Higa in Honolulu in 1966. The chain now has twenty-four locations in Hawaii. (The first one on the mainland is planned for Las Vegas; it was originally set to open at the end of 2020 but construction was delayed because of the coronavirus pandemic.) Zippy's is known for its variety of comfort food dishes that are unique to Hawaii, including loco moco. Zippy's also includes Napoleon's Bakery, which sells fresh pastries for dessert, including the famous Apple Napples. But the chili is Zippy's signature dish. It's served over rice or with fries and cheese. It can even be served in loco moco, with the chili replacing the gravy, and in omelets, burritos, or hot dogs. The chili is so popular,that the chain sells over one hundred tons of the stuff every month. Just think of the amount of rice that's served with the chili.

"We Thought Kings Ate It"
. . . .
When there was fresh, hot rice, my mom would often make *tamago kake gohan.* I loved this so much! Especially when you mixed it all up and it was a delicious mess of raw egg, *shoyu,* and rice. I'm sure that when she first introduced it, she said "raw egg on rice," but we heard "Royal Rice" so we thought kings ate it, and this is what it was called for the duration of our childhood.

Jane Miyahara

There's one last rice dish that I have to mention, which isn't so much a Japanese thing as a Japanese American thing: gravy over rice, especially at Thanksgiving! Yes, it's a cross-cultural fusion dish, but one I had growing up in Japan, when my dad made the Thanksgiving turkey while my mom cooked salmon for herself. Today, Erin and her family do the same—save the salmon part. Yes, we also have gravy on the turkey and on the mashed potatoes. But my favorite part of the holiday meal is tasting the gravy in a mouthful of rice. Seriously.

That's how adaptable, and marvelous, rice is!

8
Sweet Dreams
Desserts from Manju to Mochi Ice Cream

Food in Japan has been championed over the years as "health food" by the rest of the world. After all, Japan has the highest number of centenarians per capita on the planet, over 86,500 in 2021—you don't live to be over one hundred by eating nothing but fast food and candy, right?

Some of that thinking is based in logic: So many Japanese live to a riper old age than the rest of us because of their lifestyle, which includes their diet. Green tea, fish, seaweed, tofu, and smaller portions (no Big Gulp soft drinks, as just one example). But Japanese also walk more than Americans do. A lot more. Some of us in the US might be good about working out at the gym or riding bikes or rock climbing or hiking all over creation. But not most of us. Some of us might eat tofu and lots of veggies. Some of us might be vegetarian or maybe even vegan. But not most of us.

That being said, I can say with certainty that Japanese food isn't all healthy and good for you.

There's a lot of fried foods, just for starters. A lot. Tempura, *korokke* (the Japanese word for croquet, breaded and fried mashed potatoes and meat), tonkatsu (breaded pork cutlet), and karaage (fried marinated chicken). And Japanese love their sweets. That includes a huge diversity of sugary goodness (or badness), from candy to cakes and pastries and donuts, to the sugary sweetness that permeates so many Japanese sauces and marinades: teriyaki, for example, and the many variations of okonomiyaki or yakisoba sauce, which are a sweeter variation of Worcestershire sauce.

Candy then and now

Let me start with my childhood and the sweet memories I have of candies and other sweet treats. There's an entire new generation of Japanese candies that weren't available when I was a kid in Tokyo. The fruit-flavored Hi-Chews for one, and the many brands of gummy fruits for another (how do they get their Muscat grape flavor so spot-on, as if I'm really biting on a green grape?). In the drinks department (I'll address this more in the next chapter), the popular soda Ramune didn't exist when I was a child. Kit Kat chocolate bars, which are well liked in the US, are a cult object in Japan. Since Kit Kats were launched in Japan in the seventies, I didn't know about them until I came to America and first had the boring old regular milk-chocolate versions. When I was growing up in Japan, the most memorable confections I stuffed my face with were different versions of caramel.

My most vivid candy memories are of Morinaga Caramel, individually wrapped creamy, soft milk caramels sold in a slim, yellow box, adorned with a flowery, Art Nouveau decoration. It's an artifact of its time—it was first sold in 1913, and the package hasn't changed at all for over a century. The company was started in 1899, and its caramel is the best-selling caramel in Japan. Morinaga was started by Taichiro Morinaga, who was born the year the American Civil War ended and traveled to the US when he was twenty-three. Upon his arrival, a friendly stranger gave him a fateful gift: a piece of candy. He had never had candy before, probably just traditional sweets and pastries. It inspired Morinaga to learn how to make candy, and after returning to Japan in 1899 he sold sweets from a street cart until he saved enough to open a shop, which paid tribute to his inspiration in its name, The Morinaga Western Confectionary Shop. His iconic caramels were a hit, and by 1918 Morinaga had started manufacturing candy, the first in Japan to make and sell Japanese chocolate.

"Never Called Me Names Again"

. . . .

When I was in second grade, one of the boys in my class called me a Nip. I hadn't heard that term before, so I had no idea whether it was good or bad, but given the tone, I knew it probably wasn't good. I came home to ask my mom about it. She didn't have a strong reaction, but called his mother and asked if we could have a play date. The mother agreed, and he came to the house after school. It was weird having him there, but we hung out, and adjusted ourselves to this new dynamic. Pretty soon, my mom brought out afternoon snacks of Oreos and Kool-Aid. Chad was very surprised that we ate "American" food and devoured the cookies. After that, he was my fiercest support and he never called me names again. I always am thankful for the way this was handled.

Jane Miyahara

The company's best-known candy in the US today is Hi-Chew, morsels of fruit flavor that have the chewy mouthfeel of gum but dissolve so you don't have to spit out and otherwise dispense of the wad after you're done with it (who hasn't stuck a used piece of gum underneath a school desk top?). They're similar to a softer Starburst, with unique flavors including açaí, kiwi, and the most recent addition, dragonfruit. Hi-Chews got a boost in the US when Japanese baseball pitcher Junichi Tazawa was signed to play with the Boston Red Sox in 2012. When he was asked to supply the team with gum, he added some of his favorite candy from Japan, Hi-Chews. Instead of gnawing on gum on the mound, he started a fad with teammates, who liked the treats too and demanded buckets of Hi-Chews on the bench. The candy became so popular with Americans—starting with baseball fans—that Morinaga made sponsorship deals to provide the candy to other MLB teams and eventually opened a factory in North Carolina that employed ninety people to produce Hi-Chews. It used to be something you had to seek out in Asian supermarkets. Now, Hi-Chews are a mainstream American favorite available everywhere!

Another memorable caramel was made by the Ezaki Glico. Though its logo is just the name in English written in a simple script, even today, lots of people would recognize the brand's famous sign: a running man on a track with arms raised as if he'd just run through the ribbon for a gold medal. The iconic logo is one of the first amazing neon (or now LED) signs tourists see when they visit Osaka's famous Dotonbori shopping and dining district. A version of Glico's sign has graced the spot since 1935. Glico chose the running man as the mascot for its caramel in 1922. The reason? The founder (and candy inventor) Riichi Ezaki had added glycogen, a form of glucose from oysters, to the candy, which he claimed gave a person the energy to run "300 meters in a single piece."

I grew up with Glico's running man, but the company's biggest seller today is Pocky, simple biscuit sticks covered with chocolate and other confection flavors. The original chocolate Pocky was launched in 1966, the year my family moved from Japan to the US, so I missed the treat. In 1971 the company added an almond flavor and then strawberry in 1977.

Another favorite candy was Miruki ("Milky") by Fujiya, a chewy caramel variation made of sweetened condensed milk. The company claims the milk is from Hokkaido, which is famous for the best dairy products in Japan, so the milk candy was marketed as a healthy product for mothers to give children. Umm, right.

Like the other candies I enjoyed, Milky had a distinctive package, or rather a mascot that adorned every package. Peko-chan was a big-eyed little girl with pigtails, perpetually licking her lips because the candy was that good. Fujiya started as a confectionery store in Yokohama, which was opened in 1910 and established a reputation for its cakes. Today the company operates around one thousand cake shops throughout Japan.

The girl, Peko-chan, was first used as a symbol in 1950, and the next year, when the Milky candy was first sold, Peko's lesser-known boyfriend Poko was introduced. Lesser known in the US anyway— both characters were granted the first-ever three-dimensional trademark by Japan's patent office.

These Japanese candies aren't always easy to find in US supermarkets, but they're available in any Japanese grocery store and many Asian supermarkets, or online.

Conversely, the British-born Kit Kat crossed the Pacific in 1973. Sinc then, there have been over three hundred different flavors of Kit Kats, including the first classic Japanese version, green tea. Seasonal and special flavors have included cherry blossom mochi, edamame (really), Hokkaido roasted corn, Okinawa sweet potato, and dozens and dozens more. There's even a sake flavor. The most extravagant? A single Kit Kat bar (Kit Kats normally have two skinny bars connected side-by-side) wrapped in gold leaf. Kit Kat stores selling all the current flavors are located in tourist hotspots like airports. So if you ever go to Japan, be sure to bring back boxes of unusual Kit Kat flavors to show off. But don't give them away for Halloween—that would be a waste!

Sweets and confections

I didn't grow up just eating candy—Japan has an amazing history of sweets that aren't just the typical American dessert fare.

Wagashi is a general term for traditional confections that date back to the Edo period, when the sugar trade with China made the sweet stuff a common ingredient, at least for the higher economic classes and the samurai, who, in this era of relative peace, turned to cultural pursuits. Wagashi covers dozens of fancy and not-so-fancy treats, mostly sweet but not all (*senbei*, the savory, shoyu-coated rice crackers, are considered wagashi). Some wagashi take so much work and preparation that they are almost like tiny, bite-sized works of art.

They might be *manju*, a filled confection made of wheat flour, or mochi, steamed or baked pastries made of the familiar sticky rice cakes. Or they might be *dorayaki* or *monaka*; the first are pancake-like cookies with *anko*, sweet bean paste, between them, and the second has anko sandwiched between two wafer-like cook-ies. There are a variety of similar sweet morsels based on this idea, like *ningyoyaki*, or literally, "grilled dolls," small pieces of anko-filled shells shaped like animals, pagodas, lanterns, or even char-acters, like the anime cat Doraemon. Another, more traditional version is the *taiyaki*, cooked in a mold to look like *tai*, or sea bream, but, of course, tasting nothing like fish; the fish-like shell is made of pastry and inside is anko. There are famous taiyaki shops in Japan, including one in Tokyo's Ginza shopping district, which have sold only taiyaki for generations.

Another sweet wagashi is called *dango*, small plain balls of chewy mochi on a skewer that are grilled and then dipped in a sweet-and-savory shoyu-based sauce.

Anmitsu is sort of like a traditional Japanese fruit salad with cubes of *kanten*, or agar-agar jelly, which is made from a type of algae, similar to a clear, harder-textured Jell-O, and anko paste or whole red beans in a fruit nectar.

You can take out the confection altogether and make red beans into a sweet soup called shiruko. I grew up with shiruko thanks to my mom, who made it every New Year's Day—it must have been a wonderful treat in her freezing-cold hometown of Nemuro in Hok-kaido! On one trip to Nemuro, my wife and mom and I had din-ner with my aunt and uncle at the original location of Hanamaru, the famous conveyor-belt sushi chain, where my wife Erin noticed a sign on the wall and cried out, "They have kabocha oshiruko?!" Erin doesn't speak a lot of Japanese, but she could read the sign and she was right. My aunt and uncle didn't even realize the restaurant served a delicious, sweet seasonal soup of anko and kabocha, Japa-nese pumpkin. What a way to finish off an amazing feast!

Another incredibly sweet treat I grew up with from my mom

is *yokan*, basically a block of anko or other sweetened bean paste molded with kanten into a brick of sugary heaven. My mom still loves her yokan, and I do too—growing up I used to chomp the whole brick almost in one sitting by pushing it out of its thick foil wrapper and holding it like a popsicle, instead of forming it into the dainty thin slices you're supposed to have with your green tea.

Although these confections are all still made and sold in wagashi shops in Japan, you'd be hard-pressed to find some of the fancier treats in the US outside one of the very few Nihonmachi left on the West Coast, or in a very good Japanese market elsewhere in the country.

Bread and other wheat products

Some of these traditional sweets are made with wheat flour, but bread as we know it wasn't a common food in Japan until centuries after it was introduced by Portuguese Catholic missionaries in the sixteenth century. Because rice was already such an important part of Japan's culture, and wheat was used to make udon noodles, Japanese didn't have much use for or interest in bread. But they did take the name for these baked goods from the Portuguese *pão*, which was borrowed as *pan*.

Bread may have been shared with some high Japanese officials at first, but it mostly stayed on the shelf for several hundred years, until the mid-1800s when the military decided that bread was useful to feed soldiers in the field. After Japan was opened up by American warships, the Meiji government officially approved such foreign fare as meat and curry to help Japan catch up to the rest of the world, and bread was back on the table.

Yes, we celebrated the huge importance and historical

significance of rice to Japan in the previous chapter. But the fact is, since 2014, Japanese have consumed more bread than rice. One reason is that bread is easier to eat, whether it's *shokupan*, sliced white bread that's become a staple of modern breakfasts and the ingredient that makes a sandwich a *"sando,"* or the endless variety of both sweet and savory pastries made with wheat that harken back to traditional Japanese treats. It's not like rice is going away and will be entirely replaced by bread. Some statistics show that young people seem to prefer the old ways and are eating more rice again.

But the Japanese have found amazing ways to adapt plain old white bread to suit their food culture, including their love for sweets. You think cakes and donuts are the be-all and end-all of bready desserts? Think again.

Anpan helped spark the Japanese embrace of bread, by making bread to suit the Japanese, not the Portuguese, the British, or the Americans. European breads were sour, dry, and hard—they even called one type "hardtack." The bread that was introduced to Japan was more of a biscuit or a cracker, which suited the European sailors on long voyages—it's probably what Frodo Baggins ate on his journey to Mordor in the Lord of the Rings trilogy.

But in 1869 Yasube Kimura, the owner of an eponymous bakery in Tokyo's Ginza district, Kimuraya, invented a way to make bread that suited the Japanese palate. He was inspired by *daifuku*, sweet red bean paste inside a soft, round mochi. He found a way to make a new confection with bread on the outside and anko on the inside, while the bread remains soft and chewy.

The secret was to add yeast made with rice *koji*, the same rice mold that is used in making sake, soy sauce, and miso, to the wheat flour. He called his creation anpan, anko bread, and now his family sells 10,000 anpan a day at his original Ginza shop and another

WAGASHI FOUND STATESIDE: (*top left*) Fugetsu-Do in Los Angeles's Little Tokyo has been selling mochi and other Japanese confections since 1903. (*bottom left*) A typical scene of enjoyment at San Francisco's Benkyodo, where one could find all manner of mochi and *manju* confections. The diner and sweets shop sadly closed in 2022.

GLICO RUNNING MAN: (*above*) Although a caramel candy might not be the best food to help you win a race, the giant mascot makes for an impressive sight over Osaka's Dotonbori.

Tokyo location (run by the fourth generation of Kimuras). The sweet pastry is so popular that it even inspired a nationally loved "half-human, half-bread" mascot, Anpan Man.

As anpan caught on with Japanese consumers, so did other baked treats. Kimura's invention sparked a wave of *kashipan*, or "sweet bread." He followed up with his own variations on the genre including *jamupan*, jam bread, a bun filled with—you guessed it— jam. On the heels of these came *kurinpan*, filled with custard cream, and ultimately, one of the most popular styles of bun today, kare- pan, curry bread, which is fried and filled with curry. It's a popular street food that supposedly was invented in the 1920s by a Tokyo bakery (you can find lots of videos on YouTube that extol the amaz- ing taste of a good karepan) and, when served warm, is squishy when you pick it up. When you bite into it, you'll release steam, and the (usually mild) taste of the slightly sweet Japanese curry will spread over your palate. It's often made with beef, but not exclu- sively. Although it's fried, it usually is not too greasy, something that many Japanese fried foods share. It's a supremely satisfying snack.

This willingness to adapt bread to a variety of tastes, from sweet to savory, baked to fried, results in a vast *pan*-oply of delicious foods. You can get these buns—like sophisticated donuts that are soft and chewy, not dried out—with the above-mentioned jam, cream, and other delights. But three other types of bread snacks are worth not- ing. One is a popular sandwich of yakisoba noodles served in a hot dog bun—the *yakisoba pan*. Yes, it's double carbs if you're watch- ing your weight or blood sugar. But it's incredibly popular. Another double hit of carbs is the *korokke pan*, or potato croquette bun. Korokke are a popular street food item on their own, with potatoes and meats rolled into a patty, then breaded and deep fried (again, they're usually not too greasy), and THEN cooked into an outer layer of soft bread. Tasty, but not exactly health food.

One other curiously popular bread in Japan is called *meronpan*. From the established naming convention, you might assume this is bread that tastes like melon—say, cantaloupe—but you'd be wrong. Meronpan are larger than other "bun" breads and don't have any fillings, though some shops now cut them open and add fillings as diverse as anko, whipped cream, or ice cream (better eat it fast, especially if the meronpan is fresh out of the oven!). They're basically squishy and chewy Japanese breads, but with an unusual feature: a crunchy top that's cross-hatched in a pattern that some people say looks like a cantaloupe. I don't think so—it looks more like Godzilla's hide, or maybe a turtle's shell to be more kind. The hard top is made by layering a type of cookie dough on top of the yeasty bread beneath, and it makes for a crunch that goes great with the softness beneath. The bread was reportedly invented in 1910 by an Armenian baker who worked at the world-class Imperial Hotel. There are bakeries throughout Japan (including one in Asakusa, the crowded traditional temple and shopping area in Tokyo) where people line up at shops that sell only meronpan. For picky eaters, meronpan is increasingly baked with melon flavoring, but that just doesn't sound right to me. . . .

The king of Japanese bread is just bread itself, a loaf of good old white bread—what we might generically call "Wonder Bread" in

America. It's called shokupan, and since this is Japan, it's actually nothing at all like Wonder Bread.

Shokupan is short for *"shokuji pan,"* which can mean "bread for meals" or "eating bread." A plain loaf of bread was sold as early as the 1880s in a Yokohama shop by a British baker. But loaves of plain white bread didn't catch on right away. It took decades of tweaking by Japanese bakers to suit Japanese tastes, and then the devastation of a world war, to make shokupan not only popular, but popular enough to help bread overcome rice as the most consumed staple.

By the end of World War II, Japanese were making bread that was more like the French brioche, boasting a rich flavor and using eggs and milk to give a softer, creamier texture than other Western loaves. Shokupan is also called "Hokkaido milk bread" because dried Hokkaido milk was often used in a Chinese baking method that adds a precooked roux to the dough. The resulting bread from all this work is pillowy-soft and slightly sweet. It's cut into thick slices for toast and has become a favorite for breakfasts throughout Japan, at home and at hotels. One reason it's so popular for breakfast is that the thick slices (thicker than a typical "Texas toast" slice in US restaurants) make beautiful toast: crunchy on the outside when you bite into it, but incredibly soft and fluffy inside, like chewing on a cloud. It's perfect with butter or topped with jam, honey, or sugar. I still need my rice-and-raw-egg or rice-and-natto fix at a hotel buffet, though.

A bakery in the Asakusa district of Tokyo called Pelican was already exclusively selling shokupan during the war. But shokupan became ubiquitous for the same reason that ramen did in the postwar years. The American Occupation government sold Japan surplus US wheat, partly because Japan was suffering from a rice shortage and famine was looming, but also because American farmers just had way too much wheat on their hands. With easy access and low cost, ramen became much more than a food for Chinese immigrants in Japan, and bakeries suddenly appeared throughout the country.

Then, the Occupation government brilliantly dictated that bread should be served for school lunches. The US already had put an emphasis on American-style schools as a way to keep communism away from Japan, so feeding young Japanese nutritious food—and easing the wheat surplus at the same time—was a win-win.

The most revered sweet bread and the tastiest savory buns, and all the other handheld treats, are available at specialty bakeries in Japanese cities, towns, train stations, and airports, not to mention the tourist hotspots, supermarkets, and, of course, Japan's incredible convenience stores. You've never shopped at a 7-Eleven until you've been to a 7-Eleven in Japan (or Family Mart, or Lawson, or any of the other *conbini* throughout the country). Since 7-Eleven is owned by a Japanese company, I'm hoping some of the foods available in Japan will pop up at shops in the US. Anpan? Karepan? Yes, yes, many times, yes!

Shokupan, as well as anpan, karepan, and many other Japanese breads, may not yet be available at your friendly neighborhood supermarket, but more and more Japanese bakeries seem to be opening up in the US, especially in big cities. Even here in Denver, there are now competing Japanese bakeries that sell not just shokupan, anpan, and karepan but other treats like Japanese donuts. An added mochi layer makes for a chewy ring of fried bread that's nothing like what you'd find here in the West. They call them "ring donuts," as they are made of connected balls of mochi-textured bread. They're available stateside at Japanese and Asian bakeries even in Denver, which is a "hooray!" for cross-cultural entrepreneurship and great news for foodies like me. But hey Dunkin'—start making them here, will ya?

One of my favorite desserts as a kid both in Japan and after we moved to the US was cream puffs, or, as my mom would say, *"shu cremu."* They were wonderfully firm, hollow pastry shells, like croissants with a crust, with a round bottom that came to a peak at the top. She would cut the pastry in half between the top and bottom and then spoon in a fabulous, rich and creamy custard, before replacing the top and sprinkling powdered sugar over it. I thought it looked like a dreamy snow-capped mountain top, and eating it was just out of this world. She stopped making it years ago, but I still vividly remember how special her cream puffs were.

Cream puffs are a French confection first baked by a royal pastry chef in the 1840s. There's a Japanese company named Beard Papa's, whose logo features the smiling bearded face of a man with a knit cap on, as if he were an old-fashioned fisherman. The logo is a likeness of the company's founder, Yuji Hirota, who indeed sported a fluffy white beard. He opened a bakery in Osaka in 1999, and because of his countenance, his customers called him "Beard Papa." Voila, the store's name was born. Today there are four hundred Beard Papa's shops across the globe selling variations of shu cremu with different fillings and toppings, and several non-puff pastries, including a personal-sized cheesecake, a chocolate fondant cake, and a crème brûlée. But the cream puffs are the main attraction, no doubt. In 2004, the first Beard Papa's in the United States was opened in New York City. I first had a Beard Papa's at a counter shop near Little Tokyo in Los Angeles, and it was so good I left with a bag of them. I've also had them at Tokyo locations, including a busy spot in the Shibuya train station and a *"depachika"* (a department store basement) food hall location. They're consistently great and never fail to evoke my childhood.

Frozen treats

We've already talked about mochi and manju as some of Japan's traditional sweets. But a modern version is all-American in its invention. Or Japanese American: Frances Hashimoto, who owned the now sadly closed Mikawaya confectionery shop in Los Angeles's Little Tokyo, perfected an idea suggested by her husband, Joel Friedman, to wrap balls of ice cream with mochi. She created a way of doing just that and launched a line of mochi ice cream with seven flavors in 1994, the end result of a lot of trial-and-error mass production. When it was first sold, Mikawaya's new mochi treats accounted for fifteen percent of the novelty frozen treat market nationally in just a few months. I would guess that most Americans have still not had regular, unchilled mochi like the daifuku mochi that's filled with anko, or the hard mochi discs that are traditionally grilled every New Year and eaten with sugar and shoyu (and that cause a number of choking deaths in the elderly and children in Japan). But they know ice-cream-stuffed balls of mochi and, possibly, the mochi topping you can put on frozen yogurt alongside boba pearls and crumbled M&Ms. Mikawaya made mochi mainstream . . . if in one variation.

Mikawaya was founded in 1910 by Ryuzaburo Hashimoto, Frances's granduncle, who came from Mikawa province, which is now part of Aichi Prefecture. He made a special family recipe of mochi in his confectionery shop, which it was known for over a century. But the company's mochi ice cream is now the best-known brand of the dessert, and it's available everywhere.

Another frozen sweet treat has its roots in the Heian period of Japanese history, which ended in the twelfth century. *Kakigori* is the most basic of concepts: shaved bits of ice flavored and sweetened with syrup. It's mentioned in a book by a Heian imperial court observer, and it's still a popular dessert especially during Japan's oppressive summers. The first kakigori shop is thought to have opened in Yokohoma in 1869, thanks to the increasing availability of ice. These days, kakigori is a must-have street food during the hot summer festival season, and it's also sold in conbini, coffee shops, and restaurants.

The dish shows up in other cultures, most notably as halo-halo in the Philippines, with fruits and other ingredients added, and in China and Korea. It's become enshrined in Hawaii as "shave ice" (not "shaved" ice!) as a state favorite, with shave ice shops fighting for recognition as the best.

Kakigori was brought to Hawaii in the nineteenth century by immigrant laborers from Japan who arrived on the islands to work on the sugar and pineapple plantations. As a way to cool off, the laborers would hack at blocks of ice with their tools and then sweeten the shavings. That simple treat evolved into the elaborate shave ice of today, which can have add-ons like boba pearls, jelly, a rainbow of syrups, chocolate, red bean paste, and, of course, tiny pieces of colorful mochi—or ice cream for overkill chill.

The best-known shave ice shop in Hawaii is Matsumoto's, which opened on Oahu's North Shore in 1951 and is often cited as the top spot. They've been known to sell one thousand shave ices in one day. There are dozens of shave ice shops throughout Hawaii, but my family likes Waiola shave ice, because it's closer to the Honolulu beaches and because my father as a kid grew up just a couple of blocks away, where my grandfather owned a construction company. Reviewers give an extra thumbs-up to Waiola's *lilikoi*, or passionfruit, syrup shave ice.

I say *aloha* to that!

Nomimono
Soft Drinks, Hard Drinks, and Tea, Lots of Tea

The drink that Japan is most associated with is green tea. Its ceremonial use, its cultural traditions, and its ubiquity—have you ever heard of a Japanese person who didn't drink tea?—is unquestionable. There are a zillion variations and ways it's made, packaged, served, and sold, from high-end matcha powder to loose green tea, tea bags to refreshing, cold bottled green tea right out of a vending machine. The *chado*, or tea ceremony, is a symbol of traditional Japanese culture.

And of course green tea powder, or matcha, has become popular the world over as not only a hip, healthy drink but also as an ingredient in soba noodles, candy, cakes, cheesecakes, ice cream, donuts, and an ever-expanding list of other food.

Green tea is like wine in that wine is (basically) all from grapes, and the myriad types of tea are all from one species of tea trees or shrubs, *Camellia sinensis*. And that means all tea (except herbal teas, of course): the many types of green tea in Japan, Chinese varieties including jasmine or oolong, and the many teas from India. Yup, they're all made from the same plant.

How can so many different teas come from the same leaves? Because of a myriad of variations in growing (altitude, climate, water), harvesting (three "flushes" per year in spring, summer, and fall), and processing. Japanese teas are steamed after harvesting and then dried and processed. But how much shade they get before harvesting, how much they're steamed, and other adjustments affect the taste and color, and even the caffeine content. Trees that are shaded up to three weeks, picking only the youngest leaves, are made into the most expensive Gyokuro tea or ground into matcha powder.

Once you have your tea to brew at home, other variables come into play: the type of teapot (or, as the case may be, tea bags—tsk, tsk), how much tea you use, and the brewing temperature. The lower the temperature—to around 122 degrees Fahrenheit—the sweeter the taste. Boiling water will result in a bitter cup, but with more caffeine and the added benefit of catechins, which can help in regulating blood pressure and help with weight loss. Who knew?

Tea was imported, not surprisingly, from China, way back in the eighth century. Like so much of what we consider Japanese culture, tea was brought to Japan by Buddhist monks who encountered it during their travels through Asia. It became a drink of the emperor's household during the reign of Saga Kamino and was used by monks for religious ceremonies. Tea seeds from China were eventually cultivated in parts of Japan, with the most prized tea grown near Kyoto. During the twelfth century a Zen Buddhist monk wrote the first book about tea, *Kissa Yojoki*, or *Drink Tea and*

"We Convinced the School"

. . . .

I joined my school's Japanese National Honor Society, where our biggest yearly event was Japan Night, hosted by the club to share various aspects of Japanese culture. Junior and senior year, I was co-president with one of my longtime friends. This put the two of us in charge of primary planning for Japan Night, which acted as a fundraiser for our Japanese student teacher each year. Alongside tea ceremony, *ikebana*, video games, a raffle, and anime playing on TVs in the gym, we decided to sell rice balls, sushi, and miso soup. Somehow we convinced the school to allow us to obtain our food handler's licenses, and lend us the school kitchen for the day so we could make all the food for the evening.

Cay Fletcher

Prolong Life, in which he proposed that drinking tea could be helpful for a host of health reasons, including simple indigestion and heart disease ("because the heart loves bitter things"). Tea began to catch on in Japan, but mostly with the samurai class and at the elite levels of society.

By the 1500s, tea was a part of the lives of all Japanese, of all social levels. But *chanoyu* or chado, the tea ceremony that we're familiar with today, was developed as a Zen Buddhist ritual and became the province of top samurai, daimyo, and officials.

During the sixteenth and seventeenth centuries, an early version of the tea ceremony became an important part of diplomatic ceremonies, as Japan slowly became a unified country. Central to the tea ceremony, matcha, the ground powder of the best green tea leaves, picked after being covered for the final weeks of its ripening, was created. It has a sweeter, stronger flavor and a deeper green color.

Today, the ceremony, during which every step and movement

is choreographed, so that you have to hold the cup a certain way and the ladle must be placed exactly right, is treated more as a traditional art than a religious or political ritual. My mom took classes in chanoyu from a master in Denver, who set up a special tea room in the basement of her suburban home. The same woman taught *ikebana*, flower arranging, and gave lessons on how to play the *koto* and *shamisen*. I took some shamisen lessons from her but never really learned how to play American bluegrass music with it, which was my goal.

Growing up, I drank a lot of tea. It was hot tea back then, not so much the dizzying variety of bottled teas available these days. As with the explosion of bottled water in the US, bottled tea is available everywhere in Japan as well as in Asian groceries and now supermarket chains across America. Back then, I don't remember drinking tea with ice in it unless it was Lipton or, more likely, barley tea (*mugicha*), which is wonderful iced as a thirst quencher. We probably did have iced green tea during the hot humid summer, but mostly I remember drinking fresh-brewed hot green tea (*sencha*), roasted green tea (*hojicha*, my mom's favorite), and green tea with toasted rice (*genmaicha*).

Green tea isn't an exotic Japanese product anymore. Even Dunkin' Donuts serves green tea (including an iced sweet green tea), and the chain's "Dunkin' Refreshers" drinks claim to be "made with B vitamins and energy from green tea." Starbucks, the king of coffee, also sells a line of green tea in its shops (though "Emperor's Clouds & Mist" seems like a corny, exoticized throwback to early interaction between Japan and the West).

Not only has green tea in its more familiar forms become a common sight throughout the US, the premium version of green tea, matcha, has become part of the American culinary and beverage vocabulary in recent years. Dunkin' Donuts and Starbucks both sell a matcha latte.

Matcha, of course, is a popular ingredient in any number of (mostly sweet) foods including cakes and cookies, candy and pastries. It's incredible to think of the heart of traditional Japanese culture—the soul of the tea ceremony!—today being a mainstream ingredient of Western food culture.

Drinks, bottled and canned

These days, in Japan there is such a vibrant culture of vending machines, serving everything from burgers and hot dogs to steaming bowls of ramen, regional snacks to ice cream desserts, that almost any drink you can imagine (and some that you probably can't) is available in a vending machine, somewhere. You can get hot or iced coffee, soft drinks both Japanese and Western, bottled water, fruit drinks, and of course, lots and lots of tea.

Vending machines now even sell canned tonkotsu ramen soup from the global ramen chain Ippudo, which pops out of the machine hot. In fact, there are more than two million beverage vending machines in Japan, out of more than four million vending machines overall. The country was the first to produce coffee in a can, reflecting the importance of the vending machine market there.

One of the most common brands of bottled tea in Japan is Ito En, both in vending machines and konbini convenience stores, and it's the most familiar brand in the US. The company started in 1966 as Frontier Tea Corporation. It grew and processed its teas for wholesale and for specialty shops where tea was sold in bulk, by weight. It began selling tea in small packages aimed at consumers so people could buy it in markets and grocery stores. The company changed its name to Ito En in 1969. In the seventies it pioneered the use of vacuum packaging to keep tea fresh, then in the eighties invented the first canned green tea and changed the name of its sencha to Oi Ocha, which is its best-selling brand of tea.

Ito En expanded its corporate footprint to America in 1987 by opening Ito En USA in Hawaii. The company hasn't slowed down since: In the nineties Ito En sold the first bottled green tea in plastic bottles—the purposeful product design for the bottles evokes the traditional bamboo water flasks that had been used in Japan for centuries. Along with its packaged dried tea and matcha powder, Ito En today uses about a quarter of the tea grown in Japan.

In addition to tea, Japan has a love affair with coffee. Not just the Starbucks-style coffee poured by baristas, but canned coffee, sold in vending machines. There are coffee shop chains today, including Starbucks, throughout the country, but for decades coffee shops, called *kissaten*, were more like American diners, with homey yoshoku food and cups of java. Coffee beans first came to Japan in 1877 via laborers working in Brazil. But really, when I was growing up, Japanese were still tea drinkers. Most Japanese adults I knew, including aunts and uncles, drank Taster's Choice or Nescafe instant coffee for a caffeine fix stronger than what tea could provide. Our family must have sent a hundred jars of Taster's Choice over the years from the US to family and friends in care packages.

After beverage cans were invented in the 1930s, beer was sold in cans in both the US and Europe. But the Japanese were the first to put coffee in a can in 1965. That brand didn't last, but in 1969 the Ueshima Coffee Company, better known as UCC, began selling coffee with milk in a can. Japanese technology marched on and in the early seventies Pokka Coffee introduced a vending machine that could sell hot or cold drinks. Other popular canned coffee brands include Boss, which uses American tough-guy actor Tommy Lee Jones in a long-running series of hilarious television commercials. No wonder canned coffee is a hit in Japan.

Then there's the matter of soft drinks. When I was a kid in the late-fifties, early-sixties Japan, I didn't grow up drinking what American kids did.

Sure, I could get Coca-Cola when I went to school. A feature of my bicultural childhood, my brother and I went to school on base, but we lived off-base in a Japanese neighborhood.

I actually don't remember ever tasting a Pepsi (even today, Coke drinks seem to be much more prevalent in Japan than Pepsi). I never even saw a Dr. Pepper, or Orange Crush, or A&W Root Beer.

Then there's Ramune, a popular soft drink in Japan that has been making inroads into the US market since 1987, when its parent company, Sangaria, opened a US plant in Torrance, California. Ramune, Sangaria's main product, is a carbonated drink in a unique glass bottle and has a long history that reaches way back to 1884. That's when Alexander Cameron Sim, a British pharmacist living in Kobe, introduced a fizzy drink he initially called "*mabu soda*" (marble soda) because the bottle had a glass marble in its top that sealed in the bubbles. Tise bottle, however, had a history that went farther back than Sim and had nothing to do with Japan.

Hiram Codd was a British inventor and engineer who in 1870 invented a glass bottle that was sealed with a marble in its neck, kept in place by an indentation at the bottle's shoulder. He designed the Codd Bottle specifically for mineral soda water, which was a popular drink in England. The idea caught on in other parts of the world, including in India for a brand of soda and, in 1884, Japan, thanks to fellow Brit Sim. The bottle is no longer used except for India's Banta drinks and Sim's soda. The name mabu soda was eventually changed to Ramune, a Japanese pronunciation of "lemonade"—even though the "lemon-lime" flavor was just sweet and didn't taste like lemonade.

In the century-plus since, Ramune has become hugely popular in Japan, especially during the summer season's myriad of festivals, as a fun way to ward off the oppressive heat. Early on, Ramune caught the attention of the public when it was advertised in one of Japan's national newspapers as a way to prevent cholera. It's been sold in fifty-seven flavors over the years, from plain cola and typical fruity variations like peach, cherry, mango, and lychee to unexpected, yet very Japanese, tastes like chili oil, curry, octopus, corn potage, and wasabi. McDonald's in Japan even sold a seasonal summer McShake in a generic Ramune flavor in 2020, a reflection of the drink's ubiquitous popularity in the country.

There was no marble with the shake, unfortunately, but if you buy a glass bottle of Ramune (there are more conventional aluminum bottles available with twist-tops), it's fun to push down the marble with the built-in plunger and hear the marble clinking around while you drink!

I did drink chocolate milk in school (though being Asian and

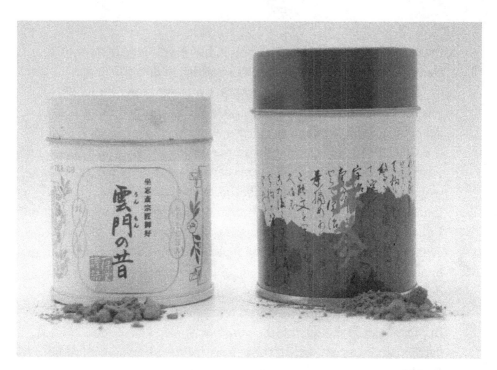

NOMIMONO: (*top left*) Matcha powder is everywhere nowadays: in lattes, cakes, and candies. But it's an essential part of the traditional Japanese tea ceremony, or *chanoyu*. (*bottom left*) Tea being served at Tokyo Suki-yaki in San Francisco, seen here as it appeared in a 1950s postcard. The photo was provided by Tamiko Wong, whose mother appears in the photo. (*above*) Although it needed a rebrand for American audiences, Calpico has become a common and popular drink in the US.

not used to Western dairy drinks, I rarely had plain milk), but I preferred it with lots of chocolate if I was using a powder like Hershey's. I don't remember Ovaltine, the American chocolate-flavored powder for milk.

I suppose I must have had Kool-Aid, made by mixing a packet in a pitcher of water and adding sugar, because, well, that was an all-American drink that was sold in the commissary, the military supermarket on base. Frozen orange juice too. But seriously, my liquid diet was very Japanese.

One very Japanese drink that's begun to appear across the US isn't even a soft drink or a variant of tea: Yakult. Pronounced "yah-koo-ru-toh," Yakult is a sweet probiotic drink sold in tiny, 2.7-ounce plastic bottles that tastes like a yummy liquid yogurt. It's promoted as a daily supplement for people to add healthy bacteria to the gut's microbiome, which in recent years has become a popular topic of health and fitness regimens.

Yakult was first sold in 1935 after the company's founder, a scientist named Minoru Shirota, cultured a strain of *Lactobacillus casei*, a "good" bacteria, that he named after himself. Five years later he launched the drink in small glass bottles, starting in Fukuoka and then marketed to the rest of Japan. In the 1960s Yakult launched door-to-door home delivery by "Yakult Ladies" who pushed carts of the drink through neighborhoods. It took until 1994 for Yakult to be introduced to the United States, and since 2014 it's been manufactured in a US factory in California. Yakult is now available in Japanese and Asian groceries and some big national supermarket chains across the country. The plastic bottle with the red foil top was first sold in 1968, and it's been joined by a low-calorie, blue-topped version that uses an extract of stevia leaves as sweetener.

Yakult got a big boost in sales in 2018 from *To All the Boys I've Loved Before*, a hit Netflix movie about a young Asian American student's romance woes. Yakult makes an uncredited cameo (the label doesn't show but viewers recognized the small bottle and red label and foil cap) in a scene where the main character, Laura Jean, watches as a boy she likes, Peter Kavinsky, drinks a "Korean yogurt smoothie." That quick flash was enough to spike the company's stock by almost three percent.

I remember drinking the original glass bottle Yakult, which I considered a version of yogurt, when I was a kid running around Tokyo neighborhoods. I liked the sweet, slightly tart taste. I never thought of it as a type of health food, or I probably would have ignored it!

One popular Japanese drink shouldn't be a surprise: It's *tonyu*, better known as soy milk in the West. Here, soy milk is a recent addition in supermarkets, a beverage that's a natural follow-up to the popularity of tofu and edamame. It's available now in grocery stores next to almond, coconut, and oat milk in sweetened and unsweetened varieties. But in Japan, soy milk is as mainstream as cow's milk and comes in more than fifty flavors as far-fetched as cola and the seasonal hit cherry-blossom-infused soy milk. Kikkoman, the company Americans are familiar with as the biggest brand of soy sauce, is, perhaps not surprisingly, one of the biggest manufacturers of tonyu in Japan.

I don't remember drinking a lot of tonyu as a kid, though. What

I drank the most, and craved constantly, was much less healthy: Calpis. That was my favorite Japanese soft drink, and it still is, under the Westernized name Calpico.

It's still sold as Calpis in Asia. But even though it's pronounced "Ka-roo-pi-soo" in Japanese, Americans simply pronounced it as if it was spelled "Cow-piss." An unfortunate brand name. The name of the drink has been changed to Calpico for the Western tongue, but the flavor is still the same.

Calpico (I'll call it by the name used in the States) is a cultured milk drink that has a slightly tangy taste like yogurt. It's sweet, but not cloyingly sweet, and it's marketed as healthy. Its origins go back more than a century. The creator of Calpico, Kaiun Mishima, was visiting Mongolia in 1904 and was fascinated by the locals' affection for a form of cultured milk that was made by fermenting milk with lactobacilli (a common bacteria that's also an ingredient in yogurt, beer, cocoa, pickles, and lots of other foods). The drink tasted refreshing and left Mishima feeling invigorated.

In 1919 Mishima launched Japan's first lactic acid beverage, which he heralded as helping digestion and control metabolism.

By the 1960s, Calpico was sold in concentrated form, packaged in brown glass bottles wrapped in white crepe paper with a blue polka-dot pattern. That design still evokes sweet childhood memories for me. When my mom wasn't looking, I would sneak drinks of the super-sweet concentrate right out of the bottle.

We moved to northern Virginia in the mid-1960s when I was eight years old. Calpico wasn't available in any American stores, though I recall seeing it in the Japanese grocery store in Washington, DC, where my mom shopped for supplies every week. When we moved to Colorado in the 1970s, we found Calpis at Pacific Mercantile, the Japanese supermarket in the new Sakura Square, the "tiny Tokyo" block of downtown Denver. Over the decades, the name changed in Japanese and Asian markets in the US from Calpis to Calpico.

Since then, a carbonated Calpico soda has been added to the product line. An array of fruit flavors—mango, lychee, strawberry, and white peach, both pre-mixed and in the original concentrate—are now sold in plastic bottles and cartons.

I won't lie—as an adult, I have been known to buy Calpico concentrate and still gulp it straight out of the bottle. I don't do that anymore (my doctor would kill me if she ever found out), but I do still enjoy me some refreshing (diluted) Calpico when I'm thirsty for something cold, smooth, and sweet.

And now, the California-based American arm of the Calpico operation has doubled down on fans' loyalty to the drink in all its variations. They've made Calpico available in some of the country's largest national supermarket chains (like Kroger's King Soopers in the Denver area), and they've launched an Amazon store just for Calpico.

It's cool to think that such an iconic drink from my childhood has finally gone mainstream in America.

Beer, wine, and liquor

For the older crowd there's alcohol. And Japanese grownups like their alcohol. Even though a third of Japanese (and other East Asians) have alcohol intolerance, it doesn't seem to stop most from drinking. Their drink of choice is beer, even though sake, like tea, is the drink more associated with traditional Japanese culture.

I don't drink alcohol because I'm allergic. I never quite enjoyed the buzz because I got a very strong reaction even sipping half a beer in my college days. My face turned bright red, and my body got splotchy after drinking, to the point that even in high school, when I would go out and drink with friends, my mom could always tell. I'd sneak quietly into the house very late at night, and my mom would be up and waiting in the living room. "You drinky?" she'd accuse in her charming strong accent. "Uh, no mom, we just drove around and went to the diner for some milkshakes," I'd stammer in reply. "No, you drinky!" she'd conclude when she saw my face. Busted.

So I've always been a cheap date, and the designated driver when going out with friends.

My dad on the other hand, who also flushed when he drank (though not as bright red as me), didn't let that stop him. He must have had enough beer since his army days for his body to develop a tolerance. And he definitely loved his beer when we lived in Japan and after we moved to the States. His favorite brand was Asahi, even though he had been stationed in Nemuro, my mom's home-town, during the Korean War and was probably as familiar with Sapporo beer, which was brewed just on the other side of Hokkaido.

Japan is best known for several brands of beer: My dad's Asahi, Sapporo, Kirin, and Okinawa's Orion are easy to find and often served in the US.

Like so many Western imports, beer was brought to Japan by Europeans, this time the Dutch traders in the 1600s. But it really caught on with Japanese drinkers during the Meiji period. The Kirin Brewing Company was founded in Yokohama in 1869, fol-lowed by Sapporo Brewery in its namesake city in 1876, and the Osaka Beer Brewing Company in 1889, which began selling Asahi Beer three years later. These three top brewers now produce their beers in the US and Canada for the North American markets.

Orion Beer is different—it's a postwar brand that reflects the US Occupation of Japan, which continued in Okinawa until 1972, even though the United States officially ended its governing of Japan as a whole in 1952. Okinawa remains home to this day to more than sixty percent of all American military personnel in Japan, with thirty-two bases on the main island. The beer launched in 1957 as part of the effort to revitalize the prefecture's economy. The name, which is pronounced "Oh-Rhee-Ohn" in Japanese, was chosen from a public contest. The Orion constellation is in the southern part of the sky and Okinawa is the southernmost part of Japan, and the three stars in the beer's logo represent both Orion's belt from the constellation and the three-star general who was commander of the US troops at the time. With its red and blue logo on a

"My Favorite Memories"

My favorite memories of Japanese food is *osechi ryori*. I remember the *tai sugata yaki* (baked sea bream) would serve as a table centerpiece to catch the good luck, and we'd eat it the day after. My Dad made the best tempura batter, which was light and tasty, maybe from adding beer. Aside from shrimp and vegetables like green beans, sweet potatoes, mushrooms, and onions, he'd sometimes surprise us with tempura oysters. His batter was always so well-seasoned that we never needed tempura dipping sauce like what's served in many Japanese restaurants today. There was always a large platter of sashimi that included *maguro*, *tako*, and fresh abalone. Many rice dishes like *maki* and *inarizushi*, *sekihan*, and *maze gohan* bursting with shrimp, sweet egg crepes, and *benishoga*. We also had my Mom's delicious sliced *chashu* and a platter of *nishime*.

Erin Yoshimura

white background, the beer's brand looks positively American—it's not surprising to see Orion sold in the US. However, as a proudly Okinawan brand, Orion isn't brewed in the West—it's exported to America.

Another alcoholic drink originally from the West that has made an impact in Japan—and is gaining a following back here in the US—is whisky. The two main distillers known for their whisky in Japan are Suntory and Nikka. Suntory was started in the 1920s, and one of its early executives founded Nikka in the 1930s. Japan wasn't known for its whisky for more than a century, and all its home-grown liquor was made for domestic consumption. However, in 2001, the single malt Yoichi whisky by Nikka won top honors from an international magazine, and since then, Japanese whiskies have been recognized internationally, even beating out Scotch whiskies in taste-testing competitions.

Japan's traditional homegrown liquor, *shochu*, can be distilled starting from a number of starches like rice, potatoes, sweet potatoes, and buckwheat, or even directly from brown sugar. Shochu originated in southern Japan, in Kagoshima, a port city at the southern tip of Kyushu, using the region's famous Satsuma *imo*, or Satsuma sweet potatoes. I tasted it once on a trip to Kagoshima and it was nasty, I thought. But what do I know, since I don't drink alcohol? I just sipped it to be polite.

Shochu has gone mainstream in Japan, with a canned brand that's available in stores (and no doubt, vending machines) under the name Chu-Hi (not to be confused with Hi-Chew candies, of course). Manufactured by Sangaria, the company that makes and distributes the Yakult probiotic drink, Chu-Hi is a modernized version of a drink that was a craze in Tokyo in the postwar 1940s. Japanese mixed their own version of the Western highball drink using Shochu, soda water, and lemon juice, and called it "Shochu Highball," which was in typical Japanese fashion shortened to *chuhai*. Sangaria's canned version is sold with either lemon or grapefruit juice.

Another Japanese liqueur that I happen to like because it's sweet, though not something I can drink much of, is *umeshu*, plum wine. If you've never tasted it, you may be familiar with it from an episode of the popular Netflix series *Midnight Diner: Tokyo Stories* (check out season 1, episode 6). Umeshu is made from green, unripened plums and rock sugar, left to steep in shochu for six months to a year. You can find brands of umeshu on liquor store shelves, but you can also make your own if you can buy the three ingredients. It makes for a great conversation starter if you have a jar of liquid on your counter with green plums soaking in it.

Going along with the Japanese love of things that are sweet and fruity, the green melon liqueur Midori has been a common aperitif or dessert sipper since it was introduced in 1964. Originally Hermes Melon Liqueur, it was rebranded as Midori (which means "green" in Japanese) and launched in 1978 at a disco-era party at the famous New York nightclub Studio 54 for the cast, crew, and producers of the film *Saturday Night Fever*—a perfectly decadent setting for a party drink!

Beer has been the most popular alcoholic beverage in Japan since the sixties, but the main drink that the world identifies with the country is sake. Some familiar brands are available in American liquor stores and restaurants in a range of prices from $8 a bottle (great for cooking) to $100 or more. There are many regional variations, and as with tea, there are rituals and specific tools associated with sake in Japan. The most familiar to Americans are the fluted ceramic containers called *tokkuri*, which are filled with sake from a bottle and then placed in boiled (not boiling) water for several minutes, and the *ochoko*, small ceramic cups to pour the sake into. That's the traditional way of drinking hot sake.

Sake is also drunk cold, in a glass or occasionally (at ceremonial events or at a nice restaurant) served in a *masu*, a wooden square cup usually made of *hinoki* cypress or sometimes lacquered wood. A masu can also be used to hold a glass for the sake; sake is poured into the glass until it overflows and spills into the box, a way of showing the restaurant's generosity with the sake.

The birth of sake isn't accurately recorded, although a Chinese text from the third century mentions Japanese drinking alcohol, and sake is mentioned in an eighth-century Japanese history. Sake became the drink of choice for festivals and religious rituals and was being brewed at both Buddhist temples and Shinto shrines by the tenth century. In the 1700s, Europeans wrote about sake for Westerners and described how the drink was made. During the Meiji period, anyone was allowed to brew sake or start a company to make and sell sake. It's illegal today to brew sake at home (home-brewed sake couldn't be taxed, so the government decided to allow only companies to brew, as that could be tracked), but the new laws have allowed sake to become mainstream enough to be known today as Japan's national drink.

Making sake seems like a simple process, but it's one steeped in millennia of traditions and adjustments. It's basically rice, water, koji (a type of mold), and yeast. The starch of the polished rice is brewed and converted into sugar by the koji, which is then fermented by yeast and turned into alcohol.

Today there are five main types of sake—*junmai, ginjo, daiginjo, honjozo,* and *namazake*—that are made with varying brewing processes and levels of rice milling.

I have to admit, I can't really differentiate the types of sake. My parents didn't drink much sake when I was a kid. They only bought bottles of sake for big celebrations like Oshogatsu. With all their friends sitting on *zabuton* mats on the floor. My dad would bring out the ceramic bottles of heated sake and pour it into the little cups. Every year I'd try a little bit, and every year I'd hate the taste. Now as an adult I don't drink it, not just because of the taste—I've tried some premium sake at events—but because I just don't drink any alcohol.

I hope my Japanese friends don't think I'm being rude. But if someone brought me a glass of Calpico, hell yeah, I'd drink that down.

Next Course

The Real Deal, Fame, and Foodies

The ongoing dynamic—struggle might be too strong of a word—for Japanese food in America today is between authenticity and appropriation, with appreciation an important marker to measure between the two extremes.

Authentic Japanese cuisine has caught on. Americans now accept sushi, ramen, and even more "exotic" dishes than just suki-yaki, teriyaki, and tempura; there's sushi in supermarkets as well as Japanese restaurants springing up all over like Starbucks. Well, maybe not quite like coffee shops on every corner, but certainly much more common than even just a couple of decades ago. With this familiarity comes creeping the inevitable fakers and cheaters—people who open Japanese restaurants because they think they can make money and ride the wave of a popular food fad.

Is sushi sold in supermarkets as good as a quality sushi

restaurant can make? No. Can gyudon taste great in a "Japanese-inspired" fast-food chain? Maybe. Can a restaurant opened by someone who hasn't been trained and raised in Japanese food culture really serve up authentic Japanese food? Yes, but I go into such places skeptical.

Maybe Japanese food is undergoing the inevitable process of evolution through assimilation into American culture, as American Chinese food has done for the past century. In fact, seeing some of the more non-traditional sushi rolls out there in Japanese restaurants that I consider unauthentic—like ones that have rice on the outside, even more outrageous than a now-tame looking California Roll, which throw together oddball ingredients and silly names like "Dragon Roll," featuring unidentifiable sashimi topped with avocado and . . . cheese!—I have to admit, I won't eat them but someone must be chowing down on them, or they wouldn't be sold.

The fact is, Japanese food in Japan has always been evolving and going with the flow—just look at the dizzying myriad of regional ramen styles, from miso in Sapporo to shoyu and shio in Tokyo to tonkotsu pork broth in Fukuoka. I once criticized a "Japanese" restaurant in Denver for serving broccoli on a bowl of ramen, but in Japan there are equally diverse variations. I don't have to like them, but I have to accept that Japanese chefs will try new ideas, whether I'll eat them or not. It's not just about tradition. Like the makers of Karami salsa, who use green chiles in place of konbu to make tsukudani, who took a family recipe that used what was available to substitute for what was not, sometimes you have to just make do and adapt.

Appropriation versus appreciation

That's where the "appreciation" part of the equation comes in.

It's tempting sometimes to think that Japanese food made by non-Japanese is automatically suspect, and I've even blogged about that in the past. But I think that anyone can make great, authentic, traditional, and modern Japanese food if they have an earnest and sincere appreciation for Japan, Japanese culture, and Japanese food traditions. It's like learning a language. You learn the rules, you communicate correctly, and at some point, you can start to embellish and improvise with the language. I know many non-Japanese who cook excellent Japanese food. And conversely, I've had plenty of average or even worse Japanese food served up by Japanese.

Japanese cuisine, after all, harkens back to traditions that are hundreds, and sometimes even thousands, of years old. Yet, Japanese cuisine has deftly absorbed and adapted outside influences for centuries. And since the mid-1800s the food culture of Japan has also displayed a voracious appetite for non-Japanese influences from the West. A lot of the food we think of as Japanese has its origins outside Japan; even the most fundamental Japanese staples like rice and tofu have their origins in China. But that's just proof that Japanese food is an amalgam of world cuisines built upon the unique culinary sources that exist in Japan's island geography.

In the US, the popularity of Japanese food and subsequent explosion of Japanese restaurants, sushi bars, and now even izakaya has led to hordes of curious diners (a good thing!) who want to get some good pan-Pacific grub but know little about what's legit and what's *"inchiki,"* fake Japanese cuisine (a bad thing). Some of the newcomers to *nihonshoku* are caught up in the fad, not the food, and may unquestioningly take the word of a hipster friend or social media influencer, who might be opinionated but actually clueless. I've seen people willing to wait an hour or more for a buzz-bound ramen shop that I've turned thumbs-down on. Not that I think I should be the definitive expert or that I'm jealous of hipster influencers, but I've walked past a long line in front of an LA restaurant and said loudly, "This place isn't as good as y'all think—there's a place down the street that's much better and there's no wait at all." I also note to myself as I amble on that I see few Asian faces waiting under the awning.

With ethnic culture as well as ethnic cuisine, there's a push and pull between authenticity, appreciation, and appropriation.

The most obvious examples of cultural appropriation are when cultural symbols of Japan are used to signify Japanese things with no appreciation of or respect for the real traditional culture.

Gilbert and Sullivan's *The Mikado* is a blatant display, since the characters, their names, their place names, and costumes are all terrible imitations of Japan through a willfully ignorant and uneducated white perspective. So is a restaurant I visited that wasn't owned by Japanese and served unappetizing Hawaiian-style poke and meh Japanese-style ramen in a setting that included giant cartoony illustrations of sumo wrestlers on the wall. Sumo should not be used as a mere prop, even if Westerners find the wrestlers a comic sight. I had the same feeling when I watched the 2000 *Charlie's Angels* film, in which Lucy Liu plays one of the crime-fighting stars. In one obnoxious scene with a "Japanese" theme, sushi is served. Women servers wear "kimono" and the entertainment includes a match between white men in blow-up sumo costumes.

"One of the Most Exciting Things"

. . . .

The Uwajimaya in Beaverton, Oregon opened in 1998, and discovering its existence was one of the most exciting things. Originally being from the Bay Area and being one of the few white kids in our area, I had grown up loving Japanese snacks. After our move to Oregon, it had been hard to find things like rice crackers or Meiji Hello Panda cookies. It was the nineties in one of the whitest states in the country, so even finding nori in the international section of the grocery store was hit or miss. Going to Uwajimaya became part of my family's regular shopping routine so we could restock the things the regular grocery store didn't carry. . . .

Everything Japanese (and Asian, since the movie appropriates Chinese and South Asian cultures too) is an at-a-glance prop to give the appearance of culture when there's only white, Eurocentric privilege on view.

Food can be twisted for marketing purposes too, to give the appearance of tradition when the food is empty of actual culture.

The "don't be fooled" mantra also applies to increasingly iconic Japanese food like Wagyu beef, with the word appearing on many phony cuts of meat that wasn't raised under strict requirements in certain approved farms in Japan. Breeding Japanese cattle with Angus might make a better cut of steak, but it won't be Wagyu. Likewise, the fact that you can find ramen everywhere doesn't mean you're getting real ramen. You might as well just buy some of the better-quality instant ramen that's available out there, even in stores such as Costco. I once asked a "chef" at a high-end supermarket who ran a sushi and ramen counter in the back, how long he cooked the pork bones for his tonkotsu ramen soup. He leaned forward conspiratorially and said, "It's a powdered mix we get from a supplier—I recommend the shoyu ramen instead."

You gotta be careful.

✳

Cross-cultural food assimilation—the ultimate act of appreciation—is a slow and inexorable process. Like modern progress, you can't stop it. Yes, paving paradise and putting up a parking lot is an outrage, but how often are these signs of "progress" stopped? In the case of food, unstoppable forces include globalization and the technology of harvesting, storing, and shipping food, whether fresh, frozen, or processed. This newfangled thing called the internet and social media have all conspired to make more people more aware of different kinds of food than just the stuff they grew up with. And that generally has been a good thing for Japanese cuisine.

As food in Japan absorbs more international influences, we'll be doing the same in America. Words like "fusion" and "evolution" will probably be more and more common when we take Japanese dishes and make them somehow American. So long as it isn't just making dishes sweeter to

. . . Japanese food is becoming more and more prevalent in Western food culture, from episodes of Binging with Babish that focus on some of the best-looking anime food to Samin Nosrat using her show's episode on salt to focus on how salt is used in Japanese cuisine and *The Great British Baking Show* having a "Japan Week." I think we're going to see more and more people interested in learning to make some of the classic Japanese dishes at home.

Cay Fletcher

suit American tastes, and it's a fusion built on authentic Japanese foundations.

Here's an example of different cultures' approach to sweetness: Kikkoman in Europe sells "sucre" soy sauce, a sweet version of soy sauce, that is hugely popular in France. When I was a kid, my mom would yell at me when I put shoyu on rice, and we were never allowed to do such a thing in a restaurant. (I still do it at home, of course!) But now, outside of Japan, it's become acceptable because of Western variations like sweet soy sauce. Remember, Kikkoman was also the brand that began marketing a teriyaki sauce for Americans in the sixties. So they've always paid attention to differing market needs. A product that probably would be ridiculed in Tokyo is a hit in Paris. *C'est la vie.*

But looking at the future of Japanese food in America, I believe that the foundations of the cuisine will continue to catch on as diners in the United States continue to be curious about the world and educate themselves on the wonderful culinary treasures of Japan. Some of these fundamentally Japanese ingredients, tastes, and dishes are already accepted here, but there are plenty more to try and embrace in the years to come, both because they taste good and they're good for you.

The new, old, and up-and-coming

The many variations of seaweed consumed in Japan—konbu, nori, wakame, *hijiki*, *mozuku* (from Okinawa), and more—have been touted as the next superfoods, which will put landlocked kale to shame. Americans have been eating nori, the dried sheets of seaweed around their sushi, for decades now. Sheets of nori that are dried in a process similar to making *washi* paper are cut into small strips called *kizami* nori (cut nori), which can be sprinkled over rice or other food as a decorative topping. Wider nori strips are even available in lots of American stores as a snack aimed at kids, with flavors added. Hint: If you see "Teriyaki" on the label of any Japanese food, know that it was made to attract non-Japanese consumers. And the pretty green tubs of seaweed salad, made with strips of wakame, have also become easy to find in US stores, even in Costco.

One common use of kizami nori is in furikake, the dried seasoning sprinkled over hot rice. There are hundreds of types in Japan, and in the US, Asian supermarkets load up entire end caps with furikake. You won't find it in restaurants yet, but in every Japanese home there are some jars of furikake hiding out in the pantry or on the table. Westerners sprinkle it not just on rice, but on popcorn. People have sprinkled dried ingredients over rice for centuries, but a bottled version of mixed ingredients was developed in the early twentieth century in Kumamoto. The company still makes the original, using powdered *iriko*, small sardines, with soy, sesame seeds, and nori.

Furikake as a manufactured product was invented by Suekichi Toshimaru, a pharmacist who wanted to make something healthy and calcium rich for people to eat on rice. Japanese at the time suffered from calcium deficiency. He dolled up his ground sardines with sesame seeds, nori flakes, and poppy seed. He called it "Gohan no Tomo," or "Friend of Rice." When a Kumamoto company bought the rights to manufacture and distribute it, it was originally sold in fluted glass flasks to help keep the furikake dry. Dozens—hundreds, maybe even thousands—of variations of furikake flavors have sprung up since the early days.

The International Furikake Association is to this day based in Kumamoto and hosts an annual "Grand Prix" to decide the best

APPROPRIATION VS APPRECIATION: (*left*) Gilbert and Sullivan's *The Mikado* is the ultimate example of Japanese culture (if you can even call the racist caricatures Japanese) being used for cheap entertainment. (*below*) A woodblock print by Yoshikazu Utagawa, an ukiyo-e artist. Ukiyo-e would go on to influence Western art movements like Impressionism when it was exported from Japan. This piece happens to depict an American ship at Yokohama.

BIG IN JAPAN . . . BUT NOT IN AMERICA: (*top left*) *Kujira*—whale meat—still has an audience in Japan, though it's on the decline. I don't see Americans lining up to eat it any time soon. (*bottom left*) *Karinto*. The unfamiliar might find the appearance unappetizing—I called it *neko no unchi* (cat poop) as a kid—but it makes for a great sweet snack.

of the wild styles from around the world. The Association was formed in 1959, and from that point on, all rice sprinkles from all brands and manufacturers, and featuring all manner of crazy seasonings, were generically referred to as "furikake." Today there's even ketchup furikake made from misshapen tomatoes that would have been tossed out by farmers. And now there are local flavors made in other countries, like a sweet, tilapia-based furikake made in Cambodia. Imagine a Texas barbecue flavor furikake here in the US. Quick, I should invent one!

A variation that's also available widely in Asian markets in America is *ochazuke*, which is basically furikake with a powdered soup base that you sprinkle over rice and add hot water or tea. It's a modern cheat on the traditional ochazuke, which was made with a variety of ingredients—bits of salmon, ikura, *tarako* and *mentaiko* (cod roe), tsukemono, umeboshi (salt-pickled plums), among others—on a bowl of rice with hot tea poured over it. My mom used to make herself ochazuke this way. She often used leftover salmon and whatever pickles she had handy, but the packaged ochazuke is a popular, quick, and easy alternative.

Like tofu, miso has been a familiar ingredient in health food stores for decades, and miso *shiru*, miso soup, has been a foundation of meals in Japanese restaurants for, well, forever. These days tubs of miso seem to be available more and more often at your neighborhood supermarket chain, not just health food grocers or Asian markets.

Along with miso soup, Japanese love to accompany their meals with a variety of tsukemono, or pickles. The term covers a huge genre of salted, fermented, preserved, and, well, pickled vegetables, both alone and in combination. Some of these side dishes are used more as condiments in small portions, and some are best saved for the brave diners who are already familiar with the dish. *Takuan*, in particular, is a pungent pickled daikon radish that can stink up a whole house even if it's stored in a sealed jar. The slices of turmeric-yellowed takuan are delicious though! The most common pickle, both in salt-pickled and dried forms, is umeboshi, pickled plums. They'll make you pucker up, but they burst with umami when you eat them and suck the pits clean. I love eating them rolled in a dish of sugar, for the full sweet and salty experience.

Tsukemono are sure to accompany your meal in any decent Japanese restaurant, so don't ignore them as just garnish. And increasingly, you can find them bagged or in jars at Japanese markets for your home meals.(or you can make them yourself).

In the 1800s, as Japanese chefs scrambled to add meat to their menus and adapt Western dishes for local palates, they developed one indispensable ingredient for all manner of meals. What the Japanese call *sosu*—"sauce"—is the result of Japanese adapting Worcestershire sauce from the British, who brought it to Japan during the Meiji period. It is a fermented mixture of vinegar, molasses, sugar, anchovies, tamarind, salt, and spices that was concocted by John Wheeley Lea and William Henry Perrins, chemists in Worcestershire, England, and first sold under their Lea & Perrins brand in 1838 (yes, it's the one on your supermarket shelf that's still sold with the tan paper wrapping around the dark brown bottle).

Japanese appropriated it and appreciated how it added what

would later be called "umami" to foods, especially the burgeoning variety of meat-based dishes, and adapted it into a uniquely Japanese variety of sauces that can be used on all manner of yoshoku. You can find it in Asian and Japanese markets today from different brands sold as "tonkatsu sauce," "okonomiyaki sauce," or "yakisoba sauce." These sauces do have different characteristics but, fundamentally, they are the same and serve the same purpose, to add a tart, sweet, and fulsome flavor to anything you pour it on. In Japan, the one generic term "sosu" pretty much covers the gamut of uses.

The influence of Worcestershire sauce was pervasive and popular. Tokyo in the years before WWII had 150 companies making sosu. Yahata Shote, a small, family-run shop in Tokyo, has been making sosu for over one hundred years, and its most famous type is its original, *usuta* (a Japanized pronunciation of "Worcester")— using sugar, salt, spices, onions, garlic, ginger, and vinegar. Generally, the Japanese brands of sosu today tend to be sweeter as well as thicker than the British original, and many sauces have apple or other fruit puree (which adds the thickness) and tomato paste (for a darker color), which makes Japanese sauce distinct from its roots.

I expect Japanese sosu to make it onto menus in some cutting-edge Japanese restaurants in the US. Sure, you always get tonkatsu sauce crisscrossed over your fried pork cutlet or karaage, but I think these sauces deserve a wider audience. How about as a Japanese steak sauce? It's not that far off from A1, and it's much cooler. Make yakisoba sauce less sweet and thinner and it can be a base for fried rice with a new twist. Eggs, burgers, . . . anything you'd put Worcestershire sauce on would be given new life with Japanese sosu.

Speaking of tonkatsu, the humble breaded, fried pork cutlet

deserves more attention as one of the fundamentals of yoshoku cuisine, which has become so accepted that it's considered truly Japanese, although still not washoku. More American restaurants should serve tonkatsu (which, as a reminder is not the same as ton*kotsu*, the pork bone soup ramen). Besides, there are Western precedents for tonkatsu that make it an already familiar dish here. Schnitzel is one, commonly made with pork, though the classic Wiener schnitzel is made with veal. Italians cook breaded thin slices of meat as *scaloppine*. The French cook a veal cutlet that's pounded, breaded, and fried and call it *escalope*. There's a wonderful family-owned yoshoku restaurant called Dorian in my mom's hometown of Nemuro in Hokkaido that serves escalope with a tomato-based demi-glace sauce instead of tonkatsu sauce.

Because of their roots in the West, I predict that yoshoku dishes—like omuraisu (chicken fried rice made with ketchup, topped with a blanket of runny omelet), kareraisu, napolitan (a postwar make-do of spaghetti with ketchup in the sauce), hambagu (hamburger steak), and korokke (deep-fried potato and meat croquettes)—will find a warm embrace among foodies in the US in the not-too-distant future. Some Japanese curry shops have already come and gone in California that I know of, but there'll be more.

The writer Elizabeth Andoh introduced the US to washoku cuisine and its traditional culture in a series of articles in *Gourmet* magazine way back in 1975. Andoh knew her subject well—she graduated from a school of traditional Japanese cuisine in Tokyo. She has since published the definitive book on the topic, *Washoku: Recipes from the Japanese Home Kitchen*. She's also written six other books.

Andoh's book didn't help washoku become mainstream in the US, but it did serve the very important purpose of educating curious foodies about the significance of traditional food in Japan.

There are restaurants in the US now serving different kinds and styles of Japanese cuisine, including even a few traditional washoku restaurants in major cities. The formats you'll more likely encounter include teishoku, or Japanese homestyle set meals, which could include traditional and yoshoku dishes, served arranged in a specific order on a tray; kaiseki, traditional multi-course meals; and *omakase*, which translates to "I'll leave it up to you"—you might be familiar with omakase if you've seen the documentary *Jiro Dreams of Sushi*. But most family-owned Japanese restaurants are bound to have a mix of washoku and yoshoku dishes or focus on one type of Japanese food like sushi or ramen.

Another yoshoku dish that's ripe for American popularity is karaage, the Japanese marinated fried chicken. Korean fried chicken has caught on—why not Japanese karaage? The bite-sized pieces of fried chicken are incredibly popular in Japan, as street food, in restaurants, and even in konbini. The konbini chain Lawson's first sold karaage in 1986, and it's become so popular that the chain now sells over 240 varieties. While American import KFC turned buckets of fried chicken into meals, konbini saw karaage as an on-the-go snack, Japan's version of a chicken nugget.

While we're on the subject of chicken, yakitori is primed for stardom stateside. The grilled skewers of chicken—all parts of the chicken—are the main event at thousands of small, family-owned yakitori restaurants. They are quick and delicious and attract hordes of salarymen and women after work, drinking and eating skewer after skewer. Yakitori would be a natural for Americans gathering after work too. The related dish of *kushikatsu*, breaded and deep-fried meats and vegetables on skewers served with a dipping sauce, would make for variety on the menu.

Japanese-style grill and hotpot restaurants are starting to appear on the US coasts. *Robatayaki* is a style of cooking seafood, vegetables, and meats over an open grill that started centuries ago in Hokkaido—a *robata* restaurant needs to open in every American city. Nabemono, or hotpots, are still the province of country-style Japanese restaurants. But its ease of cooking and open-minded embrace of all manner of meats, fish, and veggies make for a warming meal on cold nights. Some cool Japanese restaurants (one in particular in Denver, which prides itself on serving country-style Japanese) already list nabemono on their menus.

Other Japanese foods starting to appear in US restaurants include udon, one of the most traditional of Japanese noodles, which I've said for some time now will be the next wave once ramen dies down some. On the yoshoku front, the popular Japanese chain Gyu-Kaku is bringing high-level yakiniku grills to the US. The idea of grilling your own meat at a tabletop grill has been made mainstream by Korean barbecues. And, hey, yakiniku is the Japanese version of Korean *bulgogi*—so I wish Gyu-Kaku well.

There is one genre of Japanese food that is a postwar phenomenon, even though its roots predate the US Occupation. Along with the growing acceptance of ramen noodles and bread, the sale of surplus American wheat to Japan during the late 1940s boosted foods made with wheat flour. These first caught on in Osaka and include *okonomiyaki*, the savory pancake made with a batter of pork and cabbage, topped with katsuobushi shavings and kizami nori, drizzled with sosu; and *takoyaki*, pancakes molded into spheres with a piece of octopus inside, drizzled with sosu and sprinkled with flecks of nori.

Yet another food that came from the West and has been magically made extra-special is the lowly sandwich, or *sando* in Japanese. The first sando was sold in Japan in 1892 at a yoshoku food store in Ofuna Station, in Kamkaura, south of Yokohama. It was actually a box of assorted sandwiches sold as *ekiben*, a train station bento lunch. The same design is used on the boxes that contain sandwiches today. And along with train station shops, konbini, especially 7-Eleven and Lawson's stores, have perfected the art of creating sando. In Japan, sandwiches are much more than just some meat and cheese slapped on two slices of probably dry white bread. The bread in Japan is the soft, sweet shokupan, and the meat isn't always meat—you can get a surprising array of fruit and berry sandwiches in Japan. One of the most delicious meat sando is the *katsu sando*, tonkatsu cut into smaller pieces and layered between slices of shokupan, with sosu and the customary shredded cabbage in place of lettuce. It's a wonderful handheld meal. But the best sando of all makes the American version—yes, the one you grew up with—pale in comparison. The *tamago sando* that's sold in every konbini all over Japan (at least until they run out) is simply the best, most heavenly egg salad sandwich you'll ever have. We love them from 7-Eleven and Lawson's, and even the other konbini chains try to keep up.

Even the exalted late foodie Anthony Bourdain tweeted about the tamago sando: "The unnatural, inexplicable deliciousness of the Lawson's egg salad sandwich," with a photo of a package held to the phone.

*

The most common of traditional Japanese snacks, senbei, the humble rice cracker, comes in many styles, shapes, and sizes, and it's increasingly found in American food culture. For years, larger versions have been included in bags of trail mix alongside M&Ms, raisins, and nuts. Supermarket chains usually have at least one brand of rice crackers on their Asian food shelves, and every Asian grocery has a much larger selection. You can get them sweet or savory or spicy. *Kakinotane* is shaped like *kaki no tane*, persimmon seeds, and is a common feature at bars as Japan's version of beer nuts. They can be round, square, puffed up, or flat. The variations are endless. We've watched senbei being made at Asakusa in Tokyo, where a craftsman used tongs to flip a disk of rice crackers onto a grill to brown them, then dipped them into a shoyu-based sauce before sliding them into a paper sleeve and handing them over to us, still hot. If someone opened a shop making senbei fresh in the US, I swear it would be a smash hit.

Other Japanese foods on the precipice of American stardom include *kinako*, the slightly sweet, nutty-tasting ground roasted soy bean flour, which translates to "golden flour." It's commonly used to coat dango or other mochi treats, and because it's made from soy beans, already part of the American culinary landscape, it's just a matter of time until kinako becomes the "it" ingredient. (We once saw kinako ice cream in a Japanese grocery but haven't seen it since. What a great idea.)

Shiso leaves, or perilla in the West, is a refreshing herb that's used a lot in Japan but still seems unfamiliar in America. It goes hand-in-hand with tart, salty umeboshi because it has a hint of the same tartness; it can be dipped in batter and tempura-fried, made into pesto instead of basil, or used as a decorative garnish with sushi (never mind that yucky green plastic bamboo leaf stuff), and it's terrific on burgers and salads. It also makes a great ingredient for furikake. We grow it in our garden alongside basil and have it all summer, then dehydrate the last of it before the frost comes. I think it can catch on in Western produce and garden stores and with home chefs. Even Gwyneth Paltrow gives shiso a nod of approval, selling an expensive bottle of shiso perfume and an equally pricey Shiso-scented candle.

Along with all the great stuff that helps us stay excited about Japanese food in America, here are some things that I don't see catching on here. You know, though, fifteen years ago, I never would have thought unagi or uni would have become popular toppings for sushi in America. You won't find them at the supermarket sushi stand, but you will find them at any self-respecting sushi restaurant.

Pocari Sweat is a popular Japanese hydrating drink, like a healthy Calpis. It might catch on but, like Calpis's change to Calpico, I suspect it'll need a name change for the US market.

Natto is fermented soy beans, and that sounds great and healthy written out, but in real life it's stinky and slimy like snot (some Japanese Americans call it "snotto"), and just because I love it doesn't mean middle America will. However, it's worth pointing out that through the magic of science and technology natto powder is a thing, and it's available at health food stores and online. My wife had warned me, "Mark my words: powdered natto," and damned if she wasn't right.

In the same textural camp as natto, *yamaimo*, or mountain yam, and *tororo*, the grated version, are also slimy, and I don't see them gaining traction with Americans. Okra might be okay in the United States, but yamaimo takes the snottiness to new levels unless it's grilled.

Horumon will not be on the local barbecue or yakitori menu anytime soon. Also called *motsu*, it's the bits of organ meat, giblets, and other offal from cattle that would be considered "mottainai," wasteful, to throw out. It's true that Westerners might already be okay with eating liver or tripe, and that Mexican menudo is pretty darned tasty. But I'm pretty sure it'll be a stretch to get non-Japanese—hell, even many Japanese—to chow down on heart, liver, intestines, pig uterus, and, um, rectum. Beef tongue is popular in Japan, and it may be as far as Americans will go beyond steak, ribs, and roast.

I've had *basashi*, and I'm happy to say it doesn't taste like chicken. It's horsemeat, which is a traditional cuisine in Kumamoto, inspired by the tale of samurai who were trapped in Kumamoto Castle and had to eat their horses to survive. I've had basashi raw, like sashimi, and as a topping for a decent bowl of ramen. Oh, and it tastes like a stronger, sweeter version of beef, a little gamy but not unpleasant.

Kujira, like basashi, probably won't be served in American restaurants anytime soon. Like the emotional weight of chowing down on My Little Pony, Kujira has a lot—a lot—of baggage, and political baggage at that. Kujira is whale meat. I had some once at an izakaya that a journalist in Tokyo took us to. I wondered why Japanese continued to eat so much of it (in actual fact, consumption of whales in Japan has gone down so much that the whaling industry there is on the brink of collapse) and decided to try it. It tasted like gamy meat—meat of an animal on land, like deer, not like fish. The best thing I can say about kujira is that the words kujira and gorilla were mashed together to name the King of the Monsters, Gojira, as he's called in Japan. That, at least, is cool.

Along with slimy textured food, Japanese have a soft spot for some stinky foods. Oden—daikon, potatoes, carrots, konnyaku, konbu, boiled egg, tofu skin, fish cake, and more, simmered in dashi soup stock—is a winter stew that fits the nabemono hotpot genre. It sounds appealing but it can be odiferous. It's actually very popular at street carts and in some konbini chains, where customers can pick out à la carte oden ingredients and pay per item.

Also along the smelly spectrum, as I mentioned earlier, is takuan, pickled daikon radish. I like it, and my wife makes it for my mom and some older Japanese friends. But it's like making kimchi at home—you can put it in a fridge in the garage, but the odor will permeate your house. Grated daikon is equally *kusai* (smelly), but it's a wonderful condiment for steak or grilled fish. It will not become the next food fad in the United States.

Ohagi doesn't smell, and it isn't slimy, but it can be visually off-putting. It's really just like daifuku—mochi with anko inside—turned inside-out. There's mochi in the middle but it's covered with the dark, thick anko. It just doesn't look . . . appetizing as a sweet by Western standards. But it's great!

And finally, there is my favorite Japanese sweet snack that will never become popular in the US, *karinto*, which is a fried wheat cracker with a dark brown sugar coating. It looks so gross that I called it *neko no unchi* ("cat poop") growing up!

I guess there are just some Japanese delicacies that are destined to never grace Westerners' mouths.

Getting in touch with Japanese food

As I write this, because of the 2020–22 coronavirus pandemic, many Japanese restaurants—especially the small, family-owned operations—may be forced to close for good, along with lots of businesses in all sectors. What a loss to our communities!

But Japanese food in general seems to be doing fine because Americans are cooking so much more at home, and Japanese recipes are in demand more than ever before. San Francisco–based Namiko Chen, author of *Just One Cookbook,* says the website traffic for her recipes, cultural information, travel blog posts, and YouTube channel have exploded since the pandemic began. And Azusa Oda, author of *Japanese Cookbook for Beginners: Classic and Modern Recipes Made Easy,* says her virtual cooking classes have also become more popular than ever before.

With more people making Japanese food outside of the restaurant setting and in their homes, more variations and adaptations will be introduced to Americans' ideas of what "Japanese food" means.

You can even have Japanese food delivered directly to your doorstep. One recent development in Japanese food is the rash of subscription services for snacks from Japan, curated and sent directly to people outside the country. US-based Bokksu (Box) was founded in 2016 and is the most visible—they sponsor many YouTube channels about Japan, and the creators spend time on each video showing off the variety of snacks in them. Sakuraco and TokyoTreat, which are owned by the same company in Japan, also offer snacks by subscription. The services start at under $50 a month, and subscribers get a package filled with seasonal sweets, candy, savory chips, and other snacks, with an emphasis on seasonal products from small, family-owned businesses that aren't available at American Japanese markets. Other subscription businesses send assortments of packaged ramen (Umai Box) or non-food packages of toys, plush dolls, craft kits, and even ceramics and fabrics.

I mentioned earlier that the internet and social media have helped to boost the awareness of Japanese cuisine today. Along with their growing viral fame—and thanks to the coronavirus pandemic—home cooking has exploded for all types of food, including Japanese cuisine. If you're not watching cooking videos on how to make authentic Japanese food, you're watching expat YouTubers in Japan traveling through the country (as the pandemic allowed), checking out the regional cuisine. And there are a slew of Japanese YouTubers who caption their restaurant experiences in English, even if they can't speak it. It's been a fascinating and fun way to learn about Japanese food.

It's also been a great way to learn about the tools to make Japanese food, from yakitori grills and special omelet pans to the plethora of incredible Japanese knives that make slicing and dicing feel fun, not just a chore to slog through.

The celebrity chefs who shine a spotlight on Japanese food, the late Anthony Bourdain, Masaharu Morimoto of Iron Chef fame, Roy Yamaguchi of the Hawaiian chain Roy's, David Chang (who helped spark the ramen revolution in America with his Momofuku restaurant), and Ivan Orkin of Ivan Ramen, have very public profiles on broadcast television, streaming services, and YouTube and other social media platforms. YouTubers including John Daub of

Only in Japan and Paolo de Guzman of *Paolo from Tokyo*, the Tabi Eats channel, the Japanese cookbook author Namiko Chen of *Just One Cookbook*, and the terrific Netflix series *Midnight Diner: Tokyo Stories*, not to mention many programs on NHK World, the Japanese public television network's English-language service, are introducing a whole new generation of foodies to Japanese cuisine.

America has always absorbed and transformed food from the cultures of its immigrant communities, which of course includes everyone but indigenous people. That's certainly been true of Japanese food. Sometimes, the evolution of Japanese food in America has been a matter of adaptation to local ingredients, because the original ingredients just weren't available here. Sometimes, it's a matter of appreciation, like when non-Japanese embrace traditional Japanese cuisine and learn how to prepare it authentically, or when people learn to love using Japanese kitchen tools for cooking, like Japanese knives. Other times, it's plain old appropriation, as when Japanese food becomes a mere marketing hook to open a restaurant, where the food doesn't have to be great or even good, and "authenticity" is barely given a thought.

But that's what America does with all cultures and all cuisines. As an Italian friend of mine pointed out when he saw I was eating spaghetti smothered in a homemade sauce that had both ground beef and Italian sausage, "It might be tasty, but this is, at best, an American concoction. You would never get ground beef and sausage served with and on your pasta dish, except for Bolognese sauce—but this isn't Bolognese. The meat would be served as a second course. You know, it's not just Asian food that gets mangled here."

But it is indeed tasty, mangled or not. So the lesson of food in America is, cultural traditions are good and important to honor, and at the same time, it's a big country with room for all kinds of variations and desecrations.

Less than a century ago, most Americans were familiar with only a sampling of Japanese cuisine: sukiyaki, teriyaki, and tempura. Today, the dishes that immediately come to mind when someone hears "Japanese food" are more likely, sushi, ramen, and mochi. It's a testament to the growing sophistication of peoples' palates and the impact of globalization. Social media have become such an embedded part of our lives and cross-cultural curiosity has become so effortless that foreign cuisine is no longer so exotic or scary or "gross." In this new world, Japanese food can be part of mainstream American dining, in diverse variations from totally traditional and authentic to totally modern and hipster to, well, totally fake and lame.

As diners, our responsibility is to know what we're eating, embrace the good stuff, and avoid the bad.

Itadakimasu! Tabemasho!

Glossary

This is a glossary of Japanese food terms. It is by no means exhaustive, but it will help guide you through their usage in this book.

aburaage: Fried tofu.

anko: A paste made from red beans (adzuki beans). It is often sweetened and used in Japanese confections.

anmitsu: A dessert of agar jelly cubes, fruit, and syrup.

anpan: Bread buns filled with *anko* paste.

basashi: Horse meat.

chado: Also known as *chanoyu*; the Japanese tea ceremony.

chashu: Japanese version of *char siu*, Chinese barbequed pork.

chawanmushi: A type of steamed egg custard.

chirashizushi: Or simply *chirashi*; an array of sashimi over a bowl of seasoned rice.

daikon: A kind of Japanese radish.

dango: Balls of mochi on a skewer, seasoned and cooked in a variety of ways.

dashi: A broth fundamental to Japanese cuisine. It is typically made by simmering *konbu* and *katsuobushi*.

donburi: A Japanese dishes served in a bowl with rice and also the name of the bowl itself.

dorayaki: A pancake filled with *anko*.

funazushi: An older kind of sushi using fish preserved in salt.

furikake: Rice seasoning. All sorts of dried, powdered ingredients can be added to shake over plain rice.

futomaki: A kind of rolled sushi filled typically with several ingredients, egg, *kanpyo*, shiitake mushroom, and cucumber to name just a few.

gaijin: A Japanese word for non-Japanese foreigners.

genmaicha: A green tea mixed with puffed rice.

gohan: Cooked rice.

gyoza: Japanese fried dumplings.

gyudon: A kind of *donburi* with thinly sliced beef.

gyunabe: A dish of beef simmered in broth.

hibachi: A small charcoal grill. Often it is confused with a *teppan* in the West, a flat-top griddle.

hishio: The liquid from this older kind of fermented soy beans would go on to become soy sauce as we know it, while the solids would become miso.

hojicha: A kind of green tea with a distinctive roasted flavor.

hotate: Scallop.

ikura: Salmon roe.

inarizushi: Seasoned rice stuffed in pouches of fried tofu.

issei: A first-generation Japanese immigrant.

izakaya: A kind of Japanese restaurant with food and drinks.

jamupan: A jam-filled bun.

kabocha: A type of squash often referred to as Japanese pumpkin.

kaiseki: A multicourse dining format.

kaisendon: Sashimi arrayed over rice. The rice is not seasoned, unlike chirashi.

kaitenzushi: Conveyor-belt sushi.

kakiage: A type of *tempura* made with a variety of shredded ingredients held together in *tempura* batter.

kakimochi: Rice crackers.

kamaboko: A distinctive pink and white fish cake.

kanpyo: Dried, shredded calabash gourd.

kansui: An alkaline liquid used in making ramen noodles.

kanten: Agar jelly. A kind of gelatin made from algae.

karaage: Japanese fried chicken.

karepan: Fried bread stuffed with curry.

kareraisu: A thick, sweet curry over rice. It is one of the most (if not *the* most) popular dishes in Japan.

kashipan: All sorts of sweet bread.

katsuobushi: Thin shavings of smoked, dried skipjack tuna.

kazunoko: Herring roe.

kinako: Roasted soy bean powder.

koji: A kind of mold important to the production of sake and *shochu* as well as miso and soy sauce.

konbu: A variety of edible kelp that is sold dried.

konnyaku: The name of the konjac plant in Japanese. Typically refers to the cake made from starch of the root.

korokke: The Japanese word for "croquette," a breaded, fried ball of mashed potatoes and meat.

kujira: Whale meat.

kurinpan: A custard-filled bun.

kuromame: Literally "black bean." It is a kind of soy bean prepared often for Oshogatsu.

lamian: A kind of Chinese noodle that gave rise to ramen.

machi chuka: Japanese Chinese food.

maguro: Tuna.

makizushi: All kinds of rolled sushi, or sushi rolls.

manju: Wheat-based *wagashi*.

matsutake: A mushroom prized in Japan. It can reach ludicrously high prices at the market, but many people forage it for free.

mirin: A type of sweet cooking wine.

mochigome: Sticky rice used to make mochi.

monaka: *Anko* paste sandwiched between wafers.

motsu: Offal.

moyashi: Mung-bean sprouts.

mugicha: Barley tea.

musubi: A Hawaiian invention. A block of rice is topped with a slice of spam, then wrapped in *nori*.

nabemono: Dishes cooked or served in *nabe*, a pot. This may be soups or stews.

natto: A kind of fermented soy bean. Its strong smell and slimy consistency is an acquired taste.

negi: A kind of Japanese green onion.

nigari: A coagulating agent used in tofu making.

nigirizushi: Or simply *nigiri*; a type of sushi of rice topped with raw fish.

Nihonmachi: A "Japan town," a location historically occupied by Japanese immigrant communities.

ningoyaki: Like *taiyaki*, but in a variety of shapes and characters.

nissei: A second-generation Japanese immigrant.

nori: A kind of edible seaweed that is used dried and pressed into thin sheets. It is used to wrap your typical sushi roll.

ochazuke: A dish of rice with green tea poured over it.

oden: A type of *nabemono* dish. Fish cakes, boiled eggs, and vegetables, like *daikon*, are stewed in a *dashi* and soy sauce broth.

okara: The byproduct of tofu making. These are the solids left over after soy milk is separated out.

okonomiyaki: A pancake of cabbage and meat, topped with *katsuobushi* and lots of sauce.

omakase: A dining format that translates to "I'll leave it up to you." Instead of ordering, the customer lets the chef choose the courses and ingredients.

omuraisu: Or "omurice" in English; a dish of fried rice and an omelet. The name is a portmanteau of "omelet" and "rice."

onigiri: A ball of rice that can be conveniently held in the hand and filled with a variety of ingredients.

oroshi: A grated condiment, often *daikon* or ginger.

osechi ryori: The kind of food served for Japanese New Year, Oshogatsu.

oshiruko: A sweet red-bean soup.

Oshogatsu: Japanese New Year.

oyakodon: "Parent and child" *donburi*, using chicken and egg.

ozoni: A type of miso soup served on New Years' Day.

pan: All sorts of bread in Japan.

panko: Japanese breadcrumbs.

poke: Hawaiian seasoned raw fish.

ponzu: A citrusy soy sauce condiment.

ramen-ya: A restaurant serving just ramen.

renkon: Lotus root.

ryokan: A kind of traditional Japanese inn. A stay there often includes fine dining along with the room.

saba: Mackerel.

saimin: A Hawaiian variety of ramen.

sake: A word for salmon in Japanese (not to be confused with the alcoholic beverage). Also pronounced "sha-kay."

sando: All manner of sandwiches in Japan.

sansei: A third-generation Japanese immigrant.

senbei: Flavored rice crackers.

sencha: Japanese green tea.

shabu-shabu: A type of *nabemono* where diners dunk meat and vegetables in broth until they are just cooked.

shira ae: Mashed tofu salad.

shirataki: A kind of noodle made from the root of the konjac plant.

shiso: An aromatic herb in the mint family that is known as perilla in English.

shochu: A Japanese spirit made from a variety of bases, including rice, barely, or sweet potato.

shokupan: Soft and fluffy Japanese white bread.

shoyu: The Japanese word for soy sauce.

shungiku: A leafy green commonly used in *sukiyaki*. Called garland chrysanthemum or chrysanthemum greens in English.

soba: A type of Japanese noodle traditionally made with buckwheat.

sosu: All manner of Japanese sauces.

suimono: A clear, savory soup.

sukiyaki: A Japanese "hotpot" dish cooked in a skillet.

sunomono: Cucumber salad.

surimi: Fish or seafood paste. Like imitation crab.

taiyaki: An *anko*-filled pastry shaped like a fish.

takoraisu: Taco rice. An Okinawan fusion dish, it is basically a rice bowl with ground beef and salsa.

takuan: A *daikon* pickle with a distinctive yellow color.

tamago kake gohan: A dish consisting of hot rice, raw egg, and *shoyu*.

tamari: An older variety of soy sauce. Unlike most *shoyu*, it doesn't contain wheat.

teishoku: A Japanese set meal.

temaki: Often called a "hand roll"; a conical sushi roll.

tempura: Ingredient fried in a light, crisp batter.

teppanyaki: Cooking done on a flattop griddle, made famous by Benihana.

teriyaki: A way of cooking, *"yaki,"* that produces a lustrous glaze, *"teri."*

tonkatsu: A breaded and fried pork cutlet.

tonkotsu: A thick, white pork bone broth used in a popular variety of ramen.

tonyu: Soy milk.

tsukemono: Preserved vegetables; pickles.

tsukudani: A side dish made by simmering various ingredienst in soy sauce until they are deeply colored and flavored.

tsuyu: An all-purpose base for soups and sauces made from *dashi*, soy sauce, mirin, and sake.

umeboshi: Salt-pickled *ume*, often referred to as Japanese plum.

umeshu: A plum wine made by infusing *ume* in *shochu*.

unagi: Freshwater eel.

uni: Sea urchin.

unohana: A dish consisting of *okara*, the soy bean solids left over from tofu making, and an assortment of vegetables.

wagashi: Traditional Japanese confections.

Wagyu: Japanese beef prized for its high fat content. A rating system is used to help identify the best quality meat.

wakame: A kind of seaweed used in salads and miso soup.

washoku: Traditional cuisine of Japan.

yakiniku: Translates as "grilled meat." Restaurants serving *yakinuki* often have you grill slices of meat yourself over a tabletop grill.

yakitori: Translates as "grilled bird." The bird in this case is chicken. *Yakitori* is cooked and served on skewers.

yokan: A sweet made from red bean paste and agar jelly.

yonsei: A fourth-generation Japanese immigrant.

yoshoku: Foods that Japan has adopted from foreign (Western) countries.

yuba: Tofu skin. Sheets of dried soy taken from the top of soy milk.

Bibliography

Blanding, Michael. "The Strange Case of Dr. Ho Man Kwok." *Colgate Magazine,* February 2, 2019.

Corson, Trevor. *The Story of Sushi: An Unlikely Saga of Raw Fish and Rice.* New York: Harper Perennial, 2008.

Farrer, James. "The Decline of the Neighborhood Chinese Restaurant in Urban Japan." *The German Journal of Food Studies and Hospitality,* no. 2 (2018): 197–222.

Gerston, Jill. "The Reasons . . ." *New York Times,* October 4, 1974.

Hofman, Regan. "How Americans Grew to Love Benihana." *First We Feast,* November 14, 2016.

Japan External Trade Organization (JETRO). "Special Report: Serving Japanese Food to the World, Aided by the Health Conscious Boom." November 2013.

Kojima, Shigeru. "The Immigrants Who Introduced Japanese Food to the Americas." *Food Culture,* no. 22, Kikkoman Institute for International Food Culture (2012): 4–11.

Lee, Jeniffer 8. *The Fortune Cookie Chronicles.* New York: Twelve, 2008.

Master Blaster. "They Just Don't Make Japanese Food Delivery People Like They Used To." *SoraNews24,* April 14, 2015.

Mishan, Ligaya. "The New Generation of Chefs Pushing Japanese Food in Unexpected Directions." *New York Times Magazine,* September 2, 2019.

Solt, George. *The Untold History of Ramen: How Political Crisis in Japan Spawned a Global Food Craze.* Berkeley, CA: University of California Press, 2014.

Spiegel, Tamio. "Yes, It Matters: Nisei Cuisine and Japanese American Identity." Discover Nikkei, October 6, 2017, http://www.discovernikkei.org/en/journal/2017/10/6/yes-it-matters/.

Wenning, Danielle. "Consuming Culture: Effects of Globalization in American Japanese Restaurants." *Honor Scholar Theses* 54, DePauw University, 2016.

Yamashita, Samuel H. "The 'Japanese Turn' in Fine Dining in the United States, 1980–2020." *Gastronomica* 20, no. 2 (May 2020): 45–54.

Japanese Food Resources

YOUTUBE CHANNELS & STREAMING WEBSITES

This is not a complete list by any means—there are lots of YouTube channels that focus on Japanese cuisine. But these are the channels I regularly view. I'm also a big fan of NHK World-Japan, which airs the food-related shows I list here.

NHK World Japan On Demand
https://www3.nhk.or.jp/nhkworld/en/ondemand/video
NHK World Japan is the English-language version of Japan's public broadcaster (the programs are also translated into other languages). They air a lot of great, entertaining, and educational series in addition to news programming, and the shows about food are always enlightening. Some feature travel by hosts to various parts of Japan, where local foods are a highlight, and others are cooking shows that show viewers how to make the foods on view. These focus often, if not exclusively, on food:

- *Dining with the Chef*
- *Japanology Plus*
- *Cool Japan*
- *Trails to Oishii Tokyo*
- *Bento Expo*

Only in Japan * John Daub
https://www.youtube.com/c/JohnDaub
John Daub is the premiere expat American YouTuber in Japan. He's been there for over two decades and films many livestreams on his companion channel, Only in Japan GO! He often spotlights food either in Tokyo, where he lives with his wife Kanae and son Leo, or on the many travels he takes all over Japan. He's also worked for years with NHK and brings a considered, journalistic approach on his main channel.

Only in Japan Go!

https://www.youtube.com/c/ONLYinJAPANGO

John Daub stays crazy busy. He livestreams day and night from Tokyo and all over Japan, and also hosts podcast-like episodes with travel updates, which he started during the pandemic to pass along the latest information about travel to Japan. His food livestreams are smart and informed with history and cultural context.

Life Where I'm From

https://www.youtube.com/c/LifeWhereImFrom

Chinese Canadian YouTuber Greg Lam lives in Japan with his wife and kids and often delves deeply into local stories (like city planning for areas of Tokyo). But he also showcases a lot of food, including authentic Japanese family meals at home and his kids' school lunches.

Paolo from Tokyo

https://www.youtube.com/c/PaolofromTOKYO

Paolo de Guzman is a Filipino American expat who posts every Friday (US time) on topics that range from a day in the life of a Japanese worker to food videos with his recommendations in Tokyo. He travels through Japan with his wife Maiko Inagaki and their son Wolfie. (Yes, he's named after the Marvel character Wolverine, and he's adorable.)

TabiEats

https://www.youtube.com/c/TabiEats

Shinichi and Satoshi have been eating their way through Japan for the better part of a decade. Shinichi also has his own channel, Shinichi's World.

Reina Scully

https://www.youtube.com/c/ReinaScully

Reina Scully is a biracial Japanese American from New Jersey living in Japan. She doesn't always post videos about food (she vlogs about her Japanese family, trips into Tokyo, and her past as an anime voice actor and critic), but when she collects food from convenience stores or Japanese snacks, she's fun to watch

Japan by Food

https://www.youtube.com/c/JapanbyFood
Shizuka Anderson is a biracial Japanese American in Tokyo who really knows her food—she's the main star of this channel, trying lots of restaurant dishes and street food throughout the country.

Tokyo Foodie Sarah

https://www.youtube.com/c/TokyoFoodieSarah
Sarah is a London-educated Japanese "salarywoman" who explores all kind of food and drink, when she's not at her day job. She's knowledgeable and communicates in flawless English slang, inviting Western viewers in to her food world.

Ai's Munchies

https://www.youtube.com/c/aismunchies
Ai sometimes joins her friends Shinichi and Satoshi for food adventure videos and posts her take separately from theirs. She's also a chef and cooks for some videos. She's well versed in Japanese culture but sometimes doesn't seem to be familiar with traditions that her foodie friends point out. Fun to watch because she's so enthusiastic.

Jennifer Julien

https://www.youtube.com/user/jenniferjulien2012
A French ex-pat in Japan, Julien was a regular on the NHK series *Tokyo Eye* and has also accompanied John Daub on many video explorations. She's familiar with the differences in cuisine even from one Tokyo district to another, and she especially knows her alcohol.

Abroad in Japan

https://www.youtube.com/c/AbroadinJapan
Chris Broad is a British-born YouTuber in Japan who seeks out both travel and food destinations across the country. He even turned his home studio into an amazingly accurate replica of a *ramen-ya* and *izakaya* from decades ago.

Ericsurf6

https://www.youtube.com/c/ericsurf6

An American from California (yes, he surfs), Ericsurf6 shoots lots of videos trying traditional and contemporary restaurants and street food. He sometimes posts cross-cultural videos of himself in Japan and his son in the US trying Japanese restaurants.

Niki Niki

https://www.youtube.com/c/NikiNikiHawaii

Shinichi of TabiEats is originally from Hawaii, and his sister Niki posts videos of food in Hawaii, sometimes along with their mother. It's always interesting to see how Japanese food translates into Hawaiian cuisine.

5 AM Ramen

https://www.youtube.com/c/5AMRamen

Frank of 5 AM Ramen is a native Tokyoite who truly knows his ramen. He should—he eats over three hundred bowls of ramen a year, after all.

Ramen Adventures

https://www.youtube.com/c/brianramen

Brian MacDuckston has written books about ramen, including a cookbook, and has been interviewed by Western media for his expertise.

Japanese Food (Facebook group started by Gilles Poitras)

https://www.facebook.com/groups/japanesefood

There are a lot of Facebook groups about Japan and Japanese food; most seem unserious and not really a source of reliable information. But Gilles Poitras is a Japan expert (and a colleague author at Stone Bridge Press), and he's sharing great links about Japanese food in this group.

Oishii desu

https://oishii-desu.com

Greg Taniguchi is a blogger and business consultant who was born in Colorado. He spent decades on the West Coast before returning to Denver and focusing his expertise and opinions on Japanese food and businesses. He posts lists of the best and most authentic food. He also has become an authority on Japanese kitchen knives, calling out companies who lie about their knives being made in Japan.

COOKING/RECIPE WEBSITES

There are so many published cookbooks, I'm not going to list them all here. Instead I'll concentrate on a handful of excellent Japanese recipe websites and YouTube channels, and add some worthwhile cookbooks. As far as books go, Namiko Chen of *Just One Cookbook* listed below has published several cookbooks from her extensive website archives that are worth owning. You can find Japanese recipes on many general-interest sites like Food Network, AllRecipes, or Delicious by searching for Japanese recipes. The following are must-bookmark web pages that offer reliable, authentic recipes.

Just One Cookbook

https://www.justonecookbook.com

I think I can safely say that Namiko Chen is the one must-know authority for Japanese cooking (and a lot of culture too). The Osaka-born, Yokohama-raised Chen (her husband is Taiwanese American, if you're wondering) has built an empire of content, which includes over a decade of recipes she's shared online, first for friends and then as a top-level website and YouTube channel. She now publishes her recipes in printed cookbooks you can order online. She posts articles on the website that put the food in context or dig into culture and history (with the help of some outside writers) of Japanese food and traditions.

Kimono Mom

https://www.youtube.com/c/KimonoMom

Moe, a former geisha-in-training, creates cooking videos aimed at helping busy wives and moms (she's now married to a restaurant executive, and the couple are raising an adorable young daughter), with easy recipes and explanations of alternatives for hard-to-find ingredients. She's also more recently been filming vlogs of her family, not just food videos.

Chopstick Chronicles

https://www.chopstickchronicles.com

Shihoko, the author of Chopstick Chronicles, lives in Australia and began posting recipes because she missed authentic Japanese food.

Jun's Kitchen
https://www.youtube.com/c/JunsKitchen
Jun Yoshizuki is a Japanese chef who juggles five separate YouTube channels (some with his American wife, Rachel), but this one is a gem for his cooking videos, which he films while the couple's cats look on.

Cooking with Dog
https://www.youtube.com/c/cookingwithdog
A dog is the constant presence for this blog, which features a woman who cooks accompanied by stuffed poodles, while "Francis" the poodle narrates in a strong Japanese accent. The series began in 2007 and showcases over two hundred recipes with a new one posted weekly.

Rie McClenny
https://www.youtube.com/c/RieMcClenny
McClenny is a Japanese chef who works with several popular YouTube food channels, including Tasty (both alone and with collaborators) and Worth It (comparing cheap and pricey versions of food). Her cooking videos are reliable sources of authentic Japanese cooking.

BOOKS ABOUT JAPANESE CUISINE

Like websites, books about Japanese food abound. Some of them are academic and don't share the passion that I have for the cuisine. Here are some that I like and have learned from:

Exploring the World of Japanese Craft Sake: Rice, Water, Earth
By Nancy Matsumoto and Michael Tremblay
Tuttle, 2022
This beautiful volume is laid out like a longform feature in a high-class magazine, with lots of engaging photos, infographics, and information galore from sake master Michael Tremblay, plus engaging human stories about the farmers, producers, and others involved in Japan's sake industry.

Rice Noodle Fish: Deep Travels through Japan's Food Culture
Matt Goulding
HarperCollins, 2015
A journey through some of the cultural communities that make up Japan's food scene, from izakaya to salarymen, the knife makers of Sakai to the pleasures of Wagyu beef.

Chop Suey and Sushi from Sea to Shining Sea
Edited by Bruce Makoto Arnold, Tanfer Emin Tunç, and Raymond Douglas Chong
University of Arkansas Press, 2018
You can guess from the imprint that this is a collection of somewhat academic essays, but the history that's told in this book is fascinating. It looks at how Chinese food came to America and how Japanese American communities have always gathered at Chinese restaurants for special events.

Bill's Quiet Revolution: A Japanese American Artisan of California Cuisine
Sam Nakahira
samnakahira.com, 2019
This is a charming, fun-to-read historical graphic novel about Bill Fujimoto, one of the sons of Monterey Market–founder Tom Fujimoto, whose efforts to sell organic produce in the 1970s brought awareness of local, farm-to-table practices to the best restaurants in the Bay Area.

Japanese Foodways: Past and Present
Edited by Eric C. Rath and Stephanie Assmann
University of Illinois Press, 2010
A thorough collection of essays looking at six hundred years of Japanese cuisine.

CPSIA information can be obtained
at www.ICGtesting.com
Printed in the USA
JSHW020158260123
36868JS00001B/1